HOW TO SELL YOUR HOME WITHOUT A BROKER

THIRD EDITION

HOW TO SELL YOUR HOME WITHOUT A BROKER

THIRD EDITION

Bill Carey
Chantal Howell Carey
Suzanne Kiffmann

John Wiley & Sons, Inc.

New York • Chichester • Weinheim • Brisbane • Singapore • Toronto

Published simultaneously in Canada.

This publication is designed to provide accurate and authoritative information in regard
to the subject matter covered. It is sold with the understanding that the publisher is not
engaged in rendering legal, accounting, or other professional services. If legal advice or
other expert assistance is required, the services of a competent professional person should
be sought.

Library of Congress Cataloging-in-Publication Data:

Carey, Bill, 1951-
    How to sell your home without a broker / Bill Carey, Chantal Howell Carey, Suzanne
Kiffmann.—3rd ed.
      p. cm.
    Includes index.
    ISBN 0-471-38881-5 (pbk. : alk. paper).
    1. House selling.   I. Howell Carey, Chantal. II. Kiffmann, Suzanne, 1942- III. Title.
HD1379.C16   2000
333.33'83—dc21   00-032479

Printed in the United States of America.

10 9 8 7 6 5 4 3

Preface

Congratulations for being one of the smart home owners who save thousands of dollars in real estate commissions by selling your own home! In 1990, when *How to Sell Your Home Without a Broker* first appeared, nearly one out of five Americans tried to sell their homes themselves according to *Consumer Reports*. In the last five years (1996–2000) nearly one out of four Americans attempted to sell their home without a broker. In the next five years (2001–2005), it is estimated that this percentage will increase to nearly one out of three selling without a broker. Why the increase? People want to put more money in their pockets and pay less money to real estate agents.

As your property value increases, so does the amount of money you pay in real estate commission. The commission is figured on a percentage of the sales price of your property and not on a percentage of your equity. However, the commission comes out of your equity dollars and can be quite substantial in actuality and percentage. For example, if your home sells for $150,000 and you owe $120,000 on the mortgage held by the lender, then you have a gross equity of $30,000.

$$
\begin{array}{rl}
\$150,000 & \text{Sales price} \\
-\$120,000 & \text{Mortgage} \\
\hline
\$30,000 & \text{Gross equity}
\end{array}
$$

How much of that $30,000 will you receive at closing? Paying the 6 to 7 percent real estate commission will greatly decrease your proceeds. Remember, the commission is figured on the sales price and paid out of your equity.

$$
\begin{array}{rl}
\$150,000 & \text{Sales price} \\
\times \quad 7\% & \text{Commission percentage} \\
\hline
\$10,500 & \text{Commission dollars} \\
\end{array}
$$

$$
\begin{array}{rl}
\$30,000 & \text{Equity} \\
-\$10,500 & \text{Commission} \\
\hline
\$19,500 & \text{Equity after commission} \\
\end{array}
$$

$$
\frac{\$10,500 \quad \text{(commission)}}{\$30,000 \quad \text{(equity)}} = 35 \text{ percent of Equity}
$$

Paying yourself the real estate commission may provide other benefits:

- Have more flexibility in financing the sale of your present home to get the price and terms you desire.
- Receive more money with which to purchase features when choosing another home: another bedroom, bathroom, a dining room, family room, spa, or pool.
- Gain more money to make upgrades in the home you buy: carpets, drapes, landscaping.
- Have more choices in financing your new real estate purchase.
- Have more money to make other investments.
- Start with more money to pay off other debts.

How to Sell Your Home Without a Broker, Third Edition, is a step-by-step system designed to save thousands of dollars for you if you have:

- Never sold a home before and know nothing about the process.
- Sold a home previously and need information in one of several areas.
- Sold a home fairly recently and want to be updated regarding specific aspects of a successful sale.

The book is designed to take you through the entire real estate transaction from a planned beginning to a profitable end. Using *How to Sell Your Home Without a Broker, Third Edition,* you can save money on real estate commissions and successfully prepare, market, negotiate, close, and wrap up the sale of your home. We have updated the third edition with the latest tax changes and have new information on using the Internet to market your home. Good selling! Good Luck!

How to Use This Book

How to Sell Your Home Without a Broker, Third Edition, is designed to work equally well for the novice, the experienced seller, and the "professional." The following list indicates which method you would probably find most useful based on your prior experience:

- Novice, if this is your first or second sale of property or you have not sold property in the last three years.
- Experienced, if you sold at least two properties previously.
- Professional, if you sold a number of properties previously.

The checklists and worksheets are keys to the successful use of this book, whatever your level of expertise. Make notes as you read of which of the techniques and forms we provide will be most helpful to you. You will find the worksheets and contracts alphabetically in Section VI, "Worksheets and Contracts." Complete the forms you will need; photocopy them if you need more than one.

Novice Seller

If this is your first or second home sale or you have not sold a home in the last three years:

1. Examine the contents before you read each chapter to get an overview.
2. Skim the chapter checklists.
3. Begin the preparations to sell your home yourself by:
   a. Reading the entire Prepare section, Chapters 1 to 5.
   b. Checking off any method you feel you may want to use in the Use column of the checklist.
   c. Skimming the checklists of the Market, Negotiate, Close, and Wrap Up sections, to see the information they provide.
   d. Getting your property ready to market, as described in the Prepare section.

4. When you have *nearly completed* your preparations, continue with this book by:
   a. Reading the entire Market section, Chapters 6 to 8.
   b. Checking off any method you want to use in the Use column of the checklist.
   c. Skimming the Negotiate, Close, and Wrap Up sections' checklists to review what techniques these sections contain.
   d. Proceeding to market your property as described in the Market section.
5. If buyers appear while you are marketing your property, prepare by:
   a. Reading the entire Negotiate section, Chapters 9 to 13.
   b. Checking off any method you want to use in the Use column of the checklist.
   c. Skimming the contents for the Close and Wrap Up sections' checklists to refresh your memory about what they include.
   d. Negotiating the sale of your property following the guidelines suggested in the Negotiate section.
6. To complete the sale of your home, continue by:
   a. Reading the entire Close section, Chapters 14 to 16.
   b. Checking off any methods you want to use in the Use column of the checklist.
   c. Skimming the contents of the Wrap Up section's checklist to devise your plan for the remaining tasks.
   d. Closing the sale of your property.
7. Wrap up the sale of your home by:
   a. Reading the entire Wrap Up section, Chapters 17 and 18.
   b. Checking off any method you want to use.
   c. Wrapping up the sale of your property.

Experienced Seller

If you have sold two or more properties before but feel you need more information about handling various aspects of the sale:

1. Skim the Contents to get an overview of the entire sales process.
2. Use the chapter checklists in the following manner:
   a. Make a check in the Read column for areas in which you need more in-depth information.
   b. Skim the checklists for the sections of the book that deal with areas in which you feel competent.
   c. Read thoroughly the sections you checked off in the chapter checklists.

    d. Make a check in the Use column for material and forms you want to use in selling your home. Complete the forms you want to use; photocopy them if you feel you'll need more than one draft.

3. Read one section ahead of the section on which you are currently working.

Professional Seller

If you have sold a number of properties:

1. Skim the chapter checklists to get an overview of the entire sales process.

2. Use the chapter checklists in the following way:

    a. Make a check in the Read column for areas in which you need more in-depth information.

    b. Skim checklists for the sections of the book that deal with areas in which you feel competent to ensure there are no other areas for which you may need additional information.

    c. Read thoroughly the sections you checked off in the chapter checklists.

    d. Note form titles and headings for material and forms you want to use in selling your home. Complete the forms you want to use; photocopy them if you feel you'll need more than one draft.

Whatever your level of experience, we are confident that this book can help you sell your home without a broker.

Contents

Chapter Checklist

SECTION I
Prepare

1

Decide on Your Goals

Your preparation to effectively sell your home yourself includes determining the goals you wish to achieve.

Step 1: Decide on Your Goals

Decide what your primary goals are before you sell your property. Knowing your goals helps you determine many of the aspects of the sale. Your goals might include:

- Deciding where and when to move.
- Selling your property quickly.
- Receiving as much cash as possible from the transaction in order to buy another home or make investments.
- Determining the lowest price you are willing to accept.
- Having a monthly income by financing part or all of the sale yourself.
- Minimizing the tax consequences of the sale.

The Goals Worksheet helps make your priorities in selling your home clear to you. Fill out the Goals/Negotiating Goals Worksheet in Section VI, "Worksheets and Contracts" as follows:

1. Write out goals you wish to achieve in selling your home under Preliminary Goals.
2. Prioritize your listed goals by placing a number to the left of each goal. Make the most important goal 1, the second most important goal 2, and so on.

3. Rewrite your goals in their order of importance on the Prioritized Goals Worksheet to provide a reference as you sell your home.

Step 2: Understand the Property Sale Variables

When you sell can affect how fast you sell your property and even how much you receive for it. Consider the time of year, interest rates, economic climate in your area, tax regulations, and condition of property as you decide when to sell.

Timing of the Sale

Some months of the year are usually deemed better for the sales of homes, as the chart called Timing Your Property Sale indicates.

Interest Rates

Interest rates obtainable by buyers at the time you sell your home may greatly influence the number of potential buyers available. When interest rates are low, the number of buyers generally increases. The number of potential buyers increases greatly if this period of low interest rates immediately follows a period of relatively high interest rates.

Economic Climate

A healthy economy in your region can be important in determining the best time to sell your home. When the area economy is good, the number of potential home buyers who feel confident enough about the future to invest in a home usually increases, and the price of homes often increases, too.

Because the number of potential home buyers generally decreases in areas experiencing an economic slump, it may be better to retain your property during these times if possible. A rule of thumb in the real estate industry is to buy low (at a low price) and sell high (at a high price). If you must sell, you have an advantage as a "for-sale-by-owner" seller because you can sell a comparable property for less than the seller, who must pay a broker a real estate commission.

Tax Regulations

Tax regulations relating to capital gains are particularly important because they may affect your timing in selling your home. More detailed information regarding both regulations is discussed in Chapter

Timing Your Property Sale

MONTH	CONDITION	POSSIBLE REASONS
January	Few buyers available.	People recovering from the holidays.
February	More buyers in marketplace.	People in areas with cold winters find things wrong with present homes and begin to look.
March	More buyers in marketplace.	Compiling tax returns, potential first-time home buyers may decide to take advantage of tax deductions for mortgage interest.
April	Demand often highest. Prices may increase if economy is good.	People begin to be interested in homes with outdoor amenities. Families with children begin thinking of finding a home to move into during summer.
May	Similar to April.	Similar to April.
June	Similar to April.	Similar to April.
July	Demand begins to diminish.	Many people take vacations. People with children want to be moved in before new school year starts.
August	Similar to July.	Similar to July.
September	Investor activity increases.	Family demand decreases. The percentage of investors increases.
October	Similar to September.	Similar to September.
November	Demand often low.	Weather is cold, and people are preparing for the holidays.
December	Similar to November.	Similar to November.

17, "Handle Taxes." Because of rapidly changing tax laws, also contact your accountant or tax preparer for more current information.

New Law

The Tax Acts of 1997 and 1998 have combined to give most of us who own homes a wonderful tax break when we sell. On the surface, not much appears to have changed. Under the old law, we could sell our home, and as long as we bought another home of equal or greater value within two years any tax we might have on the profit would be deferred. We could keep selling each home for a more expensive one every two years. Once we reached age 55, we could sell the

"Ponderosa" and take the once-in-a-lifetime $125,000 exclusion on any deferred gains and pay no tax on the profits from all those home sales.

The new law says that if you are a married couple, you can exclude up to $500,000 of gain on the sale of your home. If you are single, you can exclude $250,000 of gain on the sale of your home. Whether you are married or single, you can do this over and over again with each new home. The only requirement is that you must have owned and lived in the home two of the last five years. No once-in-a-lifetime-over-55-must-defer-the-gain malarkey.

What if you exceed the $500,000 or $250,000 thresholds? Any gains above those figures will be taxed as capital gains with a current cap of 20 percent. As you are reading this, check to see if Congress has changed anything. Be especially vigilant with regard to the retroactive features that Congress puts in tax bills. You may sell your home in June 2001 with the current tax rules in place and then have Congress change the laws in October 2001 and make those changes retroactive to January 1, 2001. That would be nothing new. You get the picture. Just pay attention.

Condition of Property

A well-maintained home that needs no repairs or improvements is most likely to be valued for the highest price. The condition of your home when real estate professionals or appraisers view your property will influence their opinions of its values.

- If you maintain your home in *excellent* condition, so that your home appears immaculate and needs no repairs or improvements, proceed to Step 3, Gather Pricing Information.
- If your home is in less than excellent condition, consider:
    1. Reading Chapter 6, "Prepare Your Property," about the cost-effectiveness of improvement, repair, and attractiveness items, then follow *either* number 2 *or* number 3.
    2. Handling whichever improvement, repair, and/or attractiveness items you decide to take care of to increase the value of your home *before* requesting opinions about its condition.
    3. Requesting opinions of the value of your home in its *current* condition.
        a. Ask each consultant how much he or she thinks your home is now worth. Also ask how much he or she thinks the value of your home would change for each improvement or repair you are considering making.
        b. Decide what to do after you hear what your consultants consider most cost-effective.

Step 3: Gather Pricing Information

The price you decide to ask for your property may be influenced by input from any number of sources. Methods may include finding out information yourself as well as asking local real estate professionals for free market evaluations. Other methods may also encompass hiring an appraiser and asking a title company for values of comparable homes.

Choose the method or methods you feel to be the most advantageous. Consider using at least six different values from at least two sources. For example, obtain three values from a title insurance company and three different values from a real estate professional.

Use the Asking Price Determination Worksheet in Section VI, "Worksheets and Contracts" (see page 9 for example) to record your findings.

1. List the address of each property.
2. Enter the number of bedrooms and baths each home contains.
3. Write the number of square feet in the living area. (Do not include the garage or basement unless it has been converted into a permanent part of the living area.)
4. Record remarks about other amenities or property condition.
5. Enter the price in the:
   - For Sale column if the property has not closed.
   - Sold column if the property has closed.

Find Information Yourself

To find information yourself, locate several houses in your immediate neighborhood that are comparable to yours that are for sale or have recently been sold. Do not comparison shop property based on square footage alone. Consider the following items when you are deciding which properties are comparable to your own:

- Physical characteristics of the property—the number of bedrooms and bathrooms; room types and layouts; size in area (square feet); special features; age; condition; architectural style; lot size, lot shape, and topography.
- Location—view, nearness to desirable community features, and distance from undesirable features.
- Financing terms—amount of down payment, type of loans (Federal Housing Administration [FHA], Veterans Administration [VA], conventional, all-inclusive trust deed), number of loans, rate of loans, terms of loans (assumable, due-on-sale, prepayment penalties, seller buy-down).

To obtain the information you want, you can ask neighbors who are selling or have recently sold, as well as those who have recently bought. You can also attend local open houses.

ADVANTAGES

- This is an inexpensive method in terms of dollars spent.

DISADVANTAGES

- Often the method is not very accurate, because sellers may exaggerate what they received, buyers may understate what they paid, and sellers of houses currently on the market often do not receive the prices they are asking.
- Some people may be offended by your questions.
- This method uses a lot of your time for questionable results.

Ask Real Estate Professionals

Many real estate professionals will provide you with a market evaluation of your home, usually at no cost or obligation.

1. Contact several real estate professionals about providing a market evaluation at no cost or obligation to you.
2. Inform them that you are selling your home yourself, but you may call them later if you decide differently.
3. Be aware that each professional will probably try to sell you on the advantages of listing your home with his or her firm.

ADVANTAGES

- Usually there is no charge for this type of information from a real estate professional.
- Obtaining the information is easy because the real estate professional does the work.

DISADVANTAGES

- Some real estate professionals inflate their estimate of the value of your house to try to obtain a listing.
- Some real estate professionals may contact you repeatedly in an effort to list your property.

Hire an Appraiser

An *appraisal* is a supportable opinion or estimate of value as of a specific date. There are many types of appraisals for different purposes, and they may yield very different values on the same property. You need a *realistic* opinion of market value.

To get the most for your money in hiring an appraiser:

- Hire a qualified appraiser. Good sources of referrals include mortgage loan brokers, officers of a bank or savings and loan where you have accounts, real estate professionals, and real estate attorneys.

ASKING PRICE DETERMINATION WORKSHEET

Name: George and Martha

Date: 10/16/00

Address: 1600 Pennsylvania Avenue

| PROPERTY INFORMATION | | | | | PRICE | |
Property Address	BRs	BAs	Square Feet	Remarks	For Sale	Sold
Source: ☐ Appraiser ☒ Neighbors ☐ Real Estate Professional ☐ Title Company						
1300 Ohio Avenue	3	2	1600	Big yard	179,000	
1400 New York Ave	4	2	1700	Pool ; Spa		205,000
Source: ☐ Appraiser ☐ Neighbors ☒ Real Estate Professional ☐ Title Company						
1300 Delaware Ave	3	2	1600	Air conditioning	185,000	
1400 Ohio Avenue	3	3	1800	Pool, spa; air conditioning	215,000	
1500 Pennsylvania Ave	4	3	1900	Pool ; Spa		215,000
Source: ☐ Appraiser ☐ Neighbors ☐ Real Estate Professional ☒ Title Company						
1700 Pennsylvania Ave	3	2	1650	Airconditioning ; spa		195,000
MY HOME						
1600 Pennsylvania Ave	3	2	1800	For Sale Air cond, pool ; spa	215,000	
MOST COMPARABLES				Sold Pool ; spa		
1400 Ohio Avenue						
1400 New York Ave						205,000

ASKING PRICE $ 210,000

- Establish in advance the fee to be charged by the appraiser.
- Emphasize that you want a realistic opinion of market value of your residence in its present condition.

ADVANTAGES

- This process can be a useful aid in determining your asking price, especially if your house is unusual.
- The method is easy because the appraiser does the work.

DISADVANTAGES

- It may cost several hundred dollars.
- The method may not be cost-effective for properties that are similar to others in the area.

Ask Your Title Insurance Company

Your title insurance company is the organization that insured the title to your home when you purchased the property. To discover the identity of the company, check the certificate of title insurance you received when you purchased the property.

Title insurance companies usually are happy to provide at no charge information regarding similar properties that have sold recently in your neighborhood.

- Tell the title insurance company that you are selling your home yourself.
- Inform the company that you plan to use its services.

ADVANTAGES

- This method is accurate, because title companies have access to reliable, up-to-date information.
- It is easy because the title company does the work.
- Usually the service is free.

DISADVANTAGES

- It provides data on actual sales prices of homes on which the sale is complete. You do not discover, however, what prices people asked or how long the home was on the market.
- You may feel you should use the title company's services when you sell your home.

Step 4: Determine Your Asking Price

After investigating the market value of properties similar to your own and filling in the Asking Price Determination Worksheet in Section VI, "Worksheets and Contracts," you are ready to determine what price to ask for your home.

1. Decide which house *for sale* is most comparable to your own.
2. Enter this value in the Most Comparables section under For Sale on the worksheet.
3. Decide which house that *sold* is most comparable to yours.
4. Fill in the Most Comparables section under Sold with this value.
5. Consider using the most comparable:
   - For-sale price as your ceiling or high price.
   - Sold price as your floor or low price.
6. Decide your asking price after judging the housing market.
   - If the price of houses for sale in your area is rising, set your asking price just below the most comparable property's for sale price from the worksheet.
   - If the price of houses for sale in your area is stagnant or declining, set your asking price just above the price of the most comparable sold property.

After finding out asking and selling prices of other homes, you may still feel that your property is worth more than comparable properties, especially if you have made significant upgrades. Avoid letting your subjective feelings about your taste and decorating influence your evaluation of your home.

After you have decided on your goals and determined an asking price for your property, you are ready to assemble your property records, as described in Chapter 2.

2

Assemble Property Records

Having your property records readily available will greatly help you complete the steps required to sell your home yourself.

Step 1: Prepare Property Records Worksheet

Understand the Reasons for Gathering Property Records

The Property Records Worksheet and property records file help you collect and organize much of the information you need to sell your home yourself, as well as the materials to calculate your income taxes.

Prepare the Property Records Worksheet

Prepare the Property Records Worksheet in Section VI, "Worksheets and Contracts," by checking the documents you need to find for your property records file.

Prepare the Property Records File

Create a large file in which you can store most documents, records, and information about your property. You may keep this file in your home. For documents of great importance that are not easily replaced or are irreplaceable:

1. Make a copy of the document for your property records file.
2. Place the original document in a safe-deposit box.

3. Write the location of the original document on the copy.
4. File the copy in your property records file.

Step 2: Collect Documents

Gather the documents you need regarding ownership, insurance, loans, capital improvements, maintenance, and fees. Consider copying items marked in this chapter with an asterisk (*) for your file and placing (or replacing) the originals in a safe-deposit box.

Ownership Documents

These documents have to do with your property ownership. Place the documents or clear copies of them in your property records file.

Closing Statement*

The closing statement is an itemized accounting given to you and the sellers at closing by the closing agent or escrow holder. This statement details receipts, disbursements, charges, credits, and prorations.

Covenants, Conditions, and Restrictions (CC&Rs)

The CC&Rs is a document that lists private restrictions on property. *Covenants* are the promises and agreements to take or not take certain actions. *Conditions* are requirements that must precede the performance or effectiveness of something else. *Restrictions* are encumbrances that limit the use of real estate in some manner.

Subdivisions in which the buyer has some interest in common areas—such as single-family homes sharing common areas, condominiums, and time-share projects—generally have CC&Rs.

Deed to the Property

The deed you received when you bought the home may be any of the following types.

*Grant Deed.** A grant deed is a document that uses the word *grant* to transfer ownership.

*Quitclaim Deed.** A quitclaim deed is a document that uses the word *quitclaim* to transfer ownership and release the grantor from any interest in that property.

*Warranty Deed.** A warranty deed is a property deed in which the grantor guarantees the title to be as indicated.

*Gift Deed.** A gift deed is a property deed given for love and affection.

*Trustee's Deed.** A trustee's deed is a document used by a trustee in a property foreclosure handled outside the court system to transfer the debtor's title to the buyer.

Sheriff's or Marshal's Deed.* A sheriff's or marshal's deed is a document used by courts in foreclosure or in carrying out a judgment. This deed transfers a debtor's title to a buyer.

Tax or Controller's Deed.* A tax or controller's deed is a document used by a state to transfer title to a grantee.

Inspection Reports

Reports by inspectors list the condition of various aspects of your property, including defects and repairs considered necessary; they might document the results of the following types of examinations.

Physical Inspection. A physical inspection includes but is not limited to structure, plumbing, heating, electrical, built-in appliances, roof, soils, foundation, mechanical systems, pool, pool heater, pool filter, air conditioner, and possible hazards.

Geological Inspection. A geological inspection is an examination by a soils engineer for potential or actual geological problems, as well as examination of records to determine whether property falls within special zones.

Pest Control Inspection. A pest control inspection checks for infestation or infection or conditions that might lead to infestation or infection by wood-destroying pests or organisms.

Title Insurance Policy*

A title insurance policy is the coverage issued to you by the title company on completion of the final title search. The insurance provided by this document protects you against claims in the future based on circumstances in the past. This policy insures you or the lender (depending on who is insured) against certain types of losses (depending on the type of coverage) if the title is defective.

Insurance Documents

These documents are evidence of coverage on your property.

Fire Insurance

A fire insurance policy is a document from an insurance company showing to what amount a property is insured in the event of a fire.

Homeowner's Insurance

A homeowner's policy protects a homeowner from liability (damages to other people or property) and from casualty (loss of or damage to the structures or personal property). This insurance covers you for the hazards listed in the policy (such as fire, flood, and landslide). Fire and hazard insurance are types of homeowner's insurance with more limited coverage.

Mortgage Insurance

Mortgage insurance provides documents revealing that your loan is insured so that whoever you designate will be able to pay any of the following:

- The loan balance if you die and have purchased mortgage life insurance.
- The monthly mortgage charges if you are totally and permanently disabled and have purchased a mortgage disability policy.
- The lender's part of the outstanding balance in the event you default, if you purchase mortgage default insurance.

Loan Documents

Loan documents are evidence of a loan. They can include any or all of the following:

Mortgage*

A mortgage is a contract in which you promise your property to secure a loan. You retain title to and possession of the property.

Trust Deed*

A trust deed is a document, used as a security device for the loan on your property, by which you transfer bare (naked) legal title with the power of sale to a trustee. This transfer is in effect until you have totally paid off the loan.

Promissory Note*

A promissory note is a written contract you sign promising to pay a definite amount of money by a definite future date.

Payment Statements*

Payment statements can be either monthly stubs or annual summary statements. Both should show your payment date, amounts applied to principal and interest, and remaining balance due.

Property Tax Statements

Property tax statements are documents that the county assessor's office mails to you as a homeowner. These statements itemize the semiannual or annual tax bill on your home and indicate the payment due dates.

Assessment Notices

An assessment notice (or reassessment) is a document sent to you by the county assessor's office to give you notice of changes in the assessed value of your property.

Improvement Notices

Improvement notices are documents sent by governmental authorities giving you notice of planned improvements such as sidewalks, curbs, and sewers. These are one-time charges.

Satisfaction of Mortgage*

A satisfaction of mortgage is a document that indicates you paid your mortgage in full.

Reconveyance Deed*

A reconveyance deed is a document filed at the county recorder's office recording full satisfaction of a debt on your home and transferring legal title from the trustee to you.

Capital Improvement Documents

Capital improvements are additions to your property that:

- Are permanent; they cannot be removed.
- Increase the value of the property.
- Have a useful life of more than one year.

Capital Improvements Worksheet

The total cost of all capital improvements is used to calculate your basis in your home for tax purposes. The Capital Improvements Worksheet in Section VI, "Worksheets and Contracts," makes it easy to collect data. In the past, the items listed on the worksheet were considered capital improvements. Check with your accountant or tax preparer for the current status of these items.

Plans and Specifications

Plans and specifications are descriptions and drawings of the improvement, including but not limited to blueprints, prepared by you or a professional.

Estimates

Estimates include all written and signed approximations of the cost of the work required that are submitted by contractors for each property improvement.

Contracts

Contracts are the agreements spelling out all terms and conditions for each property improvement signed by both you and the contractors.

Building Permits

Building permits are documents that permit building after your plans are approved by the necessary city and/or county agencies.

Inspection Records

Inspection records are notices indicating that inspections were conducted by the proper local authorities at the required points in the building process.

Payment Records

Payment records include all checks, receipts, and written ledgers indicating date, amount paid, and type of work.

Invoices

Invoices are documents that provide proof of payment for any expenses you incur related to your property improvements. Invoices could cover material costs, labor costs, and subcontractor fees.

Preliminary Lien Notices

Preliminary lien notices are documents notifying you of liens (charges on property for the payment of a debt) presented to you.

Completion Notices

Completion notices are documents you file and record with your county when your home improvement is completed. These notices place time limits for filing mechanics' liens. Store a copy of the completion notice in your file.

Lien Releases*

Lien releases (also called waivers of lien) are documents that release you from monetary liability to the person listed on the release whom you paid in full. Obtain lien releases from suppliers, subcontractors, and general contractors.

Maintenance Records

Maintenance records encompass all documents relating to general upkeep for your property, including such items as repairs to plumbing and electrical systems, garden maintenance, and painting, as well as the purchase of carpet, drapes, furniture, and appliances.

Invoices

Invoices are documents that are proof of payment for any expense you incur in maintaining your home.

Guarantees and Warranties

Guarantees and warranties are documents providing assurances of the quality of or length of usage to be expected of a product. These assurances can be of aid in obtaining satisfaction if an object or service is not as promised or if it malfunctions within given time or usage limits.

Ownership Costs

Gather information for the preceding year about costs that would be of interest to potential buyers of your property. Costs include utilities, taxes, insurance, and homeowner's association dues.

Calculate Ownership Costs

Use the Ownership Costs Worksheet in Section VI, "Worksheets and Contracts" (see page 19 for example), to gather and process the data as explained here:

1. Write the property address.
2. Enter the year for which you gathered the information on the line preceding the name of each month.
3. Record the cost for each item for which you were charged that month.
4. Add the numbers in each column to obtain a total for that column.
5. Enter the total amount for each column on the appropriate line marked Total.
6. Record the number of months represented by the figures in each column on the appropriate line beside Number of months.
7. Divide the Total by the Number of months for each column.
8. Enter the answer for each column on the line marked Average/month.

Step 3: Organize Your Property Records File

If you have not done so already, organize the documents in your property records file in the order indicated on the Property Records Worksheet in Section VI, "Worksheets and Contracts." With your documents organized this way, you can find them easily when you need to refer to them.

After you have gathered, processed, and organized all the available documents concerning your property, you are ready to estimate the financial impact of the sale of your property. This activity is the subject of Chapter 3.

OWNERSHIP COSTS WORKSHEET

Name: George and Martha   Date: 10/16/00

Address: 1600 Pennsylvania Avenue

Year	Month	Electric	Gas/Oil	Water	Sewer	Trash		Utilities Subtotal
00	January	$ 100	$ 115	$ 60	$ 35	$ 50		$ 360
00	February	95	105	55	35			290
00	March	105	110	65	35	50		365
00	April	75	95	60	35			265
00	May	75	85	65	35	50		310
00	June	75	65	70	35			245
00	July	115	40	75	35	50		290
00	August	125	30	75	35			265
00	September	110	40	70	35	50		305
99	October	105	55	65	35			260
99	November	100	65	60	35	50		310
99	December	120	95	60	35			310
Total		$1200	$ 900	$ 780	$420	$ 300		$3600
Number of months		12	12	12	12	12		12
Average/month		$ 100	$ 75	$ 65	$ 35	$ 25		$ 300

Year	Month	Assn. dues	Insur- ance	Taxes	Bond	Other Subtotal		Grand Total
00	January				$ 100	$ 100		$ 460
00	February				100	100		390
00	March				100	100		465
00	April				100	100		365
00	May				100	100		410
00	June		$ 360	$1200	100	1660		1905
00	July				100	100		390
00	August				100	100		365
00	September				100	100		405
99	October				100	100		360
99	November				100	100		410
99	December			$1200	100	1300		1610
Total			$ 360	$2400	$1200	$3960		$ 7560
Number of months			12	12	12	12		12
Average/month			$ 30	$ 200	$100	$ 330		$ 630

3

Determine Your Financial Requirements

Once you have collected the records that document the history of your property's ownership, insurance, loan, improvements, maintenance, and costs, you are ready to determine your financial requirements.

Step 1: Estimate Costs

To best understand and plan for your financial requirements, you must understand and estimate your costs.

Prepare Net Proceeds Worksheet

Use the Net Proceeds Worksheet in Section VI, "Worksheets and Contracts," to calculate approximately how much money you will have remaining after deductions for your loans, marketing costs, and closing costs. This remaining amount is your *net proceeds*. Prepare this worksheet by:

1. Entering the address of your property.
2. Recording your asking price.
3. Calling the lenders from whom you have your loans (mortgages, trust deeds, and/or home equity lines of credit) and asking:
   - How much do I owe on this loan?
   - Is there a prepayment penalty if I pay off this loan?
   - If so, what is the prepayment penalty?
4. Writing information obtained from lenders on the worksheet.
5. Entering the expenses you estimate for the following costs on the cost section of the worksheet.

Estimate Marketing Costs

Marketing costs to consider are fix-up and advertising expenses. We discuss each of these expenses briefly at this time so that you can estimate the costs involved. A more in-depth discussion of each of the items can be found in Chapter 6, "Prepare Your Property," and Chapter 7, "Advertise!"

Improvement Costs. Improvement costs are expenses for permanent additions. These additions generally add to the value of your home if they are done well and are not overimprovements. Overimproving is adding to the worth of your home beyond the reasonable market value of comparable homes in your area. If you overimprove, you may not be able to recover the cost of the work. Consider making no improvements after you decide to sell your home.

Repair Costs. Repair costs are expenditures for work that maintains your home's condition. Repairs include replacement of items, as well as restoring function to items. Repairing obvious problems generally makes your home sellable to a greater number of buyers. In their minds, buyers may exaggerate a repair that seems minor to you into a major reason for not purchasing your home. Repairs of obvious problems you are able to fix for a reasonable price are usually very cost-effective.

Outside repairs might include such things as removing or replacing plantings; or removing, repairing, or replacing outdoor structures or exterior items on your home. Inside repairs could involve repairing or replacing interior items in your home.

Do not attempt to conceal problems by making poor or cosmetic repairs. Whether or not your state has disclosure laws, you may make yourself liable to lawsuits if you make this type of repair and do not disclose significant problems.

Attractiveness Costs. Attractiveness costs are charges for items that are not repairs or improvements but make your home more appealing to buyers. Attractiveness is in the eye, ear, and nose of the beholder. If your home makes a good first impression, viewers are more likely to want to purchase it and pay top dollar.

Attractiveness costs are usually minimal to negligible. They include work you can usually hire someone to do for a minimal charge or do yourself. The costs are generally for such items as house cleaning as well as yard and perhaps pool maintenance.

Advertising Costs. Advertising costs include the expenses you incur in letting people know that your home is for sale. These charges include such items as signs and flags, classified or display newspaper advertisements, newsletter and magazine advertisements, flyers, and open houses.

Costs can vary widely depending on the advertising you plan to do and the charges for this advertising in your area. For the purposes of this estimate, consider allocating about $300 to $500 for the first week you plan to have your home on the market and approximately $100 per week for each week thereafter.

Estimate Closing Costs

Closing costs (costs of sale) are expenses over and above the purchase price in buying and selling real estate.

The closing costs typically run between 1.5 and 3 percent of the sales price, excluding any real estate commission. This percentage estimates that you will pay the usual costs that sellers in your area generally pay.

Negotiability of Costs. Your net proceeds also depend on who actually pays which costs. Costs are negotiable except for fees on VA loans. Study the Market Effect on Payment of Closing Costs chart. It explains how your closing costs may vary depending on the type of market at the time you sell your home and whether there is an excess of sellers or buyers.

Market Effect on Payment of Closing Costs		
MARKET	**EXCESS**	**YOU MIGHT CONSIDER**
Normal	Neither	Paying the usual closing costs.
Buyers'	Sellers	Paying more closing costs than usual yourself.
Sellers'	Buyers	Asking buyers to pay more costs than usual.

Costs Included. The list of costs to consider as closing costs is too long and detailed to include here or to fully factor as you calculate your estimated net proceeds. If you want to know more about closing costs, see Chapter 9, "Prepare for Negotiation."

Estimate Moving Expenses

Estimate your moving costs if you plan to move from the home you are selling. Moving costs, though not strictly regarded as expenses of selling your home, may definitely be substantial enough to be budgeted for when you sell. Moving costs depend on many factors, such as how many pounds of goods you move, how far you move, and by what method(s) you choose to move the items. If you are concerned about these costs, read Chapter 18, "Move!"

Step 2: Calculate Estimated Net Proceeds

To calculate your estimated net proceeds from your home sale on your Net Proceeds Worksheet found in Section VI, "Worksheets and Contracts."

1. Total all the items you listed as Costs against the asking price.
2. Enter this value on the line labeled Total Costs against asking price.

3. Subtract this Total of costs against asking price from the Asking price above to obtain the Net proceeds.

Step 3: Understand Financial Arrangements

Numerous methods for financing the sale of your home exist. Understanding the most commonly used methods and choosing the ones that best fit your needs can be an important part of putting money in your pocket.

Understand All Cash Offers

With all cash offers, you can receive all cash (less the costs of the sale) from selling your house. This occurs in two ways. Usually buyers put some cash down and obtain financing for the balance of the purchase price from a lender. Sometimes buyers may have enough money to buy your home outright; however, this happens in only about 4 percent of home purchases.

ADVANTAGES
- You have received all your money from the house.
- You have no further interest in the property.

DISADVANTAGES
- You may have a large tax bill to pay, depending on your financial situation.
- You may need to find a way to invest your money.

Understand Buyers Taking over Your Loan

Your participation in financing the sale of your home may make your home easier to sell. This is particularly true when mortgage money is expensive or difficult for buyers to obtain from the usual sources.

"Assumable" Loan

An "assumable" loan is an existing trust deed or mortgage that is kept at the same interest rate and terms as you agreed to when you financed the property and for which buyers become primarily liable. You become secondarily liable for the loan and for any deficiency judgment arising from it. A *deficiency judgment* is a court decision making an individual personally liable for the payoff of a remaining amount due because less than the full amount was obtained by foreclosure on the property.

Buyers may want to assume a loan on the property if the terms and conditions of the existing loan are more attractive than those on a new loan. Some VA and FHA loans are assumable loans.

If you want to allow buyers to assume your loan, consider these steps:

1. Reading your existing loan to be sure the loan is assumable.
2. Consulting a loan officer in your local bank or your attorney if you are unsure whether your loan is assumable.
3. Asking the lender of an assumable loan if the lender requires:
   - Qualification of the buyers. Buyers must prove to a lender that they can make the payments and are good credit risks.
   - Assumption fee. Lenders charge to let buyers assume primary liability for payment of the loan.
   - Renegotiation of the loan. A lender may require buyers to renegotiate the loan, so the terms and conditions differ—sometimes substantially—from the original loan.
4. Requesting that you be released from all liability if buyers assume the loan. For most assumable loans, buyers become primarily liable, but you remain *secondarily liable* for the loan and any deficiency judgment arising from it.

ADVANTAGES
- Property may be easier to sell with this loan.
- Buyers may become primarily liable for the loan.

DISADVANTAGES
- You may remain secondarily liable for the loan.
- Buyers may not want an assumable loan if the lender requires them to qualify for the loan, pay an assumption fee, and/or renegotiate the loan.

"Subject-to" Loan

A "subject-to" loan is an existing loan for which buyers agree to take over responsibility for payments under the same terms and conditions as existed when you agreed to the loan. You remain primarily liable for any deficiency judgment. The loan's name comes from the fact that buyers taking over the loan are subject to your approval. These loans are typically pre-1988 VA and pre-1986 FHA loans.

ADVANTAGES
- Property may be easier to sell with this type of loan.
- Buyers do not have to qualify for the loan.
- Escrow may be shorter because no new loan is required.

DISADVANTAGES
- You remain primarily liable for the loan if the buyers do not pay.
- You could lose a portion or all of your VA eligibility to purchase your next home.

Due-on-Sale Clause

A due-on-sale clause is a type of acceleration clause in a mortgage, trust deed, or promissory note that gives a lender the right to demand all sums owed be paid immediately if the owner of the property transfers title.

ADVANTAGES

- If you make a loan to the buyer to purchase your home, when the buyer transfers title, you get your money back sooner than you expected.

DISADVANTAGES

- You must pay off the loan during the closing.
- If you make a loan to buyers to purchase your home, when buyers transfer title, you get your money back. You cannot choose when that time will be.

Prepayment Penalty

A prepayment penalty is a fine imposed on a borrower by a lender for the early payoff of a loan or any substantial part of a loan. To find out if you have a prepayment penalty on your loan, check your loan documents. If the documents contain such a clause, you can determine what its cost is using this procedure:

1. To calculate the amount of your prepayment penalty, check your loan documents. The amount of the prepayment penalty is usually stated as a certain number of months interest in addition to the amount you owe as of that date.
2. To determine the tax implications of this punitive interest, consult your accountant or tax preparer.

ADVANTAGES

- If you make a loan to buyers to purchase your property that includes a prepayment penalty, they must pay you the fine you agreed on if they pay the loan off early.

DISADVANTAGES

- If you must pay a prepayment penalty when you sell, you will have to come up with an agreed-on amount of extra money when you may have little extra available.

Understand Buyers Obtaining New Financing

When buyers obtain new financing, they pay you the full amount of the proceeds in cash. Whether buyers obtain a conventional loan or a government-guaranteed or government-insured loan has an effect on your sale. The details of the loan (fixed rate, adjustable rate, and so on) do not affect your cash proceeds.

Conventional Loans

Conventional loans—those obtained from commercial banking institutions such as banks, savings and loans (S&Ls), or mortgage companies—are not guaranteed or insured by government agencies.

ADVANTAGES
- These loans require a shorter processing time and less paperwork.
- There are no rules requiring you to pay some of buyers' points.

DISADVANTAGES
- A larger down payment is usually required, so not as many buyers qualify for the loan.
- Interest rates are usually higher.

VA and FHA Loans

VA loans are guaranteed by the Veterans Administration. FHA loans are insured by the Federal Housing Administration. Existing VA and FHA loans are described under assumable loans earlier in the chapter. New VA and FHA loans have certain advantages and disadvantages.

ADVANTAGES
- Buyers who do not qualify for a conventional loan may be able to buy your home because of the low down payment or low interest rates.

DISADVANTAGES
- A new VA or FHA loan typically requires 30 to 45 days longer and much more paperwork to process than does a conventional loan.
- You must pay certain buyer's closing costs on both VA and FHA loans.
- You must pay points on a VA loan.

Understand Your Participation in Buyers' Financing

Your participation in financing the sale of your home may make your home easier to sell. This is particularly true when mortgage money is expensive or difficult for a buyer to obtain from the usual sources.

The *down payment* is the amount of money that you and the buyers agree should be paid or that the lender requires that buyers pay toward the property purchase before the closing. A *deposit* or *earnest money* is money the buyers present with a purchase offer as a sign of their good faith and ability to purchase your home. A deposit generally represents part of the down payment.

Weigh the advantages and disadvantages of different amounts of down payment. Decide a range of down payments within which you are comfortable selling your home.

Large Down Payments

Down payments of 20 percent or more are usually considered large. For most sellers, the advantages of requiring buyers to make a large down payment outweigh the disadvantages.

ADVANTAGES

- Large down payments enable buyers to qualify for a loan for which they might not otherwise be able to qualify.
- Buyers making bigger down payments tend to take better care of the property than buyers who have less invested.
- A large financial stake makes buyers less likely to default on the loan because of the large loss should they default.
- Such a down payment makes more money available for you to put into investments that have a higher rate of return.

DISADVANTAGES

- Large down payments give you a smaller monthly income from the sale of your property if you make the loan to the buyers yourself.
- Buyers with a large monthly income but a small down payment may not qualify to buy your home.

Small Down Payments

Down payments of 10 percent or less are generally considered small. The benefits of permitting buyers to make a small down payment may outweigh the drawbacks in some situations.

ADVANTAGES

- A smaller down payment makes it easier to sell your property because more buyers can qualify.
- It allows buyers who have a large monthly income but a small down payment to buy the property.
- A small down payment may provide you with a high return if what you are making on the loan is the highest rate of return you can get on your money at equal risk.
- This type of financing provides you with a larger monthly income if you decide to make the loan to the buyer yourself.

DISADVANTAGES

- Buyers may be more likely to default on the loan. They have less to lose.
- You could lose the whole loan amount if the buyers default and the underlying lender forecloses.

Seller Buy-Down Loan

A seller buy-down loan is financing in which the effective interest rate is bought down (reduced) during the beginning years of the loan by your contributions. You are really paying for the buyers' interest in advance. This lower interest rate usually lasts two to three years. You may increase the price to cover this additional cost. The following is an example of a seller buy-down loan:

A loan for $100,000 at 12 percent interest has payments totaling $12,000 per year.

Seller pays $3,000 for a two-year buy-down, of which:

$2,000 is applied to buyer's first year's payments.

$1,000 is applied to buyer's second year's payments.

Buyer pays on $100,000 loan:

$10,000 during first year for an effective rate of 10 percent.

$11,000 during second year for an effective rate of 11 percent.

ADVANTAGES

- More buyers may be interested in buying your house if you offer the buy-down loan.
- It enables buyers to purchase the property who might not otherwise qualify.
- You may be able to sell your property sooner.

DISADVANTAGES

- Buyers may be more likely to default because they don't have as much invested.
- If you pay buyers' interest in advance and do not increase the price, you will obtain less money from the sale.

Seller Carry-Back Loan

Under a seller carry-back loan agreement, you act as a lender to "carry back," or hold, loan notes from the buyers. These notes may be first, second, or even third loans.

ADVANTAGES

- Terms and conditions of the loan are negotiable.
- You may receive monthly income from the loan.
- You may be eligible for capital gains tax deferment.
- Buyers do not need to qualify for an institutional loan.
- Buyers do not pay loan origination fees or points, which may make them more likely to purchase your home.

DISADVANTAGES

- You may spend time and effort to qualify the buyers to ensure that they have the ability to pay.
- More time and effort is necessary to find out about any regulations that may apply in order to avoid breaking any laws.
- You may spend time, effort, and possibly money to make sure the agreement is written properly.

Consider consulting a professional, such as your attorney, before signing a seller carry-back loan agreement in order to:

- Qualify buyers to be sure that they have the ability to pay.
- Write the agreement properly.
- Inform you of any rules that may apply, such as federally required and imputed (assigned) interest rates.

All Inclusive Trust Deed (AITD, Wraparound Mortgage)

The all inclusive trust deed (AITD), also known as a wraparound mortgage, is a junior (second, third, and so on) loan at one overall interest rate used to wrap the existing loans into a package. The amount of this loan you make to the buyers is sufficient to cover the existing loan and provide additional funds for you. You make payments on the existing loans from buyers' payments. You remain primarily responsible for the loans that are wrapped. These loans are also referred to as overriding deeds of trust. The following is an example of an AITD:

Purchase price	$ 125,000
Down payment	− 25,000
Buyer's AITD at 11 percent	100,000
Buyer's AITD at 11 percent	100,000
Seller's 1st trust deed (TD) at 8 percent	− 70,000
Seller's equity	30,000
Buyer's 12-month interest on AITD to seller ($100,000 times 11 percent)	11,000
Seller's 12-month interest on 1st TD to lender ($70,000 times 8 percent)	− 5,600
Seller's return on equity ($11,000 − $5,600)	5,400
Seller's return on equity ($5,400/$30,000)	18 percent

ADVANTAGES

- The wraparound mortgage allows you more price and sales flexibility, because you do the financing.
- This may be the only practical way to sell a home where the existing loan contains a lock-in clause. A lock-in clause prohibits the prepayment of a note.
- The wraparound mortgage retains favorable terms on existing loans.

DISADVANTAGES

- You are responsible for the loans in the case of foreclosure.
- To be safe you may want to go to the effort and expense of qualifying buyers to be sure that they have the ability to pay.
- You must find out about any regulations that apply.
- You may have to pay a professional to make sure the agreement is written properly.

Consult persons knowledgeable in real estate finance to design the loan. Establishing this loan may include these tasks:

- Paying off or renegotiating an existing loan that restricts the sale or other transfer of title (alienation).
- Participating in the Federal National Mortgage Association (FNMA) Refinance and Resale Program.
- Determining what conditions constitute default.
- Preparing a realistic payment schedule to cover existing loans.
- Deciding who will set up, pay for, and administer collection procedures. (Both seller and buyers may be most protected from default if the AITD is set up so that a trustee handles all the payments and holds the AITD.)
- Writing a legally binding AITD contract.

Land Sale Contract (Conditional Sales Contract, Contract for Deed)

A land sale contract is a type of installment sale agreement that stipulates that the seller retain title to the property until the buyers perform all the conditions of the contract. Because this contract is less frequently used than other loan forms and can be quite complex, consider consulting your real estate attorney if you desire to use this form of financing.

Now that you have determined your financial requirements, you are ready to select consultants to aid you with various aspects of the sales process.

4

Select Your Consultants

Having consultants provide you with professional advice and/or services can be very useful when you sell your home yourself. The consultants you might want to consider include accountants or tax preparers, attorneys, closing agents/escrow holders, home inspectors, lenders, title insurance companies—and sometimes even real estate professionals.

Step 1: Select Consultants

Consider selecting consultants to provide services at this point, if you have not already done so, to:

- Obtain maximum benefit from the services that they offer.
- Avoid choosing a consultant or company that does not like to deal with people who sell their own homes.

As you interview these professionals, complete the worksheet for that profession that appears in Section VI, "Worksheets and Contracts."

Accountants or Tax Preparers

An accountant is a person who keeps, audits, and inspects financial records, prepares financial reports, gives tax advice, and prepares tax returns. The more complicated your financial affairs, the more you may be able to profit from consulting an accountant before you sell your home.

31

Tax preparers prepare tax returns. They can tell you about the laws regarding taxes. Consider using an accountant or tax preparer to:

- Aid you in determining financial implications of your sale.
- Help you determine possible tax implications before you sell your home.
- Prepare tax returns after you have sold your home.

Attorneys

Attorneys are people licensed to practice law. An attorney's business is to give legal advice and/or assistance, as well as to prosecute and defend causes in courts. Choose an attorney who specializes in real estate and who can guide your sale through the entire process, as needed. Hire a local attorney, because laws and local customs affecting real estate sales vary. Depending on where you live, you might consider using an attorney to:

- Write or review the purchase contract before you sign it.
- Write or review other contracts, such as leases and options.
- Hold the earnest money in a trust account.
- Qualify buyers.
- Remedy any defects in your title.
- Handle any legal complications that could prevent closing.
- Manage the closing.
- Represent you in any actions against the buyer.

Closing Agents/Escrow Holders

The closing is the final stage of a real estate transaction. It involves signing loan documents, paying closing costs, and delivering the deed. A closing agent is a person you authorize to carry out the closing process for you.

Escrow is a type of closing. In this process you and buyers deposit documents and/or money with a neutral third party, the escrow holder. You and buyers give instructions to the escrow holder to hold and deliver documents and/or money upon the performance of certain conditions. The escrow officer is the person within an escrow company with whom you will be dealing.

Consider using an escrow, although you are not legally required to do so. Because the mechanics of property transfer are fairly complex, the advantages of having an escrow are numerous:

- An escrow officer can answer many of your questions.
- Safekeeping of documents and money is handled by a neutral third party.

- The escrow agent will carry out contract terms, including:
  - Receiving and disbursing money.
  - Preparing, obtaining, and recording documents.
  - Calculating the proration of interest, taxes, insurance, and other funds.
- The system provides an assurance that all the conditions of the sale will be met before buyers receive documents and you receive funds.

Home Inspectors

Home inspectors can provide you and buyers with detailed information about the condition of your home. A home inspector first thoroughly examines the general physical condition of your property's site and structures. The inspector then submits a detailed written report on the quality and condition of its site and structures. This report usually lists what is in good repair, as well as current and impending possible problems.

Providing a physical inspection report to buyers generally makes your home easier to sell. A physical inspection report may:

- Convince buyers you are not trying to hide problems.
- Allow buyers to understand what problems they must deal with, if they buy your property.
- Convert most physical problems from contingencies to bargaining issues to be dealt with immediately.
- Aid you in filling out a real estate disclosure statement.

Lenders

Institutional real estate lenders are organizations that loan money for real estate loans. Such lenders include banks, savings and loans, thrifts, credit unions, and mortgage companies.

If you do not have the knowledge and experience to prequalify buyers (decide what buyers are able to afford), consider:

1. Finding a lender with whom you like to deal. This may be the lender who holds a loan on your present home.
2. Asking the lender to answer any questions you may have regarding financing the sale of your property.
3. Having that lender prequalify buyers for you.
4. Being sure that the prequalifying interview:
   - Is free to the buyer who is being prequalified.
   - Does not obligate buyers to that particular lender.

Title Insurance Companies

Title insurance companies issue policies of title insurance. These policies ensure that the title is free of liens (a charge on real property to pay some debt). The nature and extent of the liens depend on the type of policy purchased. In some states, a title insurance policy must be issued before you can close the sale of your property.

In some areas, title insurance companies act as escrow holders. Check with a real estate professional or title company if you are unsure about who handles the duties in your area.

Title companies often provide other services, most of which are available without charge. They usually answer questions and give explanations, provide information about properties comparable to yours that have been recently sold in your area, and deliver important documents to city, county, and lenders' offices.

Step 2: Ask Needed Questions

The Real Estate Professional Questions Worksheet in Section VI, "Worksheets and Contracts," contain some of the questions most frequently asked of professionals involved in real estate transactions. These worksheets enable you to keep track of questions to ask consultants and provide space to record their answers. The consultants' time may be expensive. Even if you are not paying for that time directly, consultants will probably appreciate your thoroughness and thoughtfulness.

1. Write an *X* in the Ask column for all questions you want to ask a particular consultant.
2. Enter any other questions in the spaces provided.
3. Write or check off the response you receive in the space provided following the question.
4. Keep sheets handy so that you can refer to them easily.

Step 3: Understand Real Estate Terms

Due to the involved nature of real estate terminology, you need to understand the definitions of some terms before you read the listing of the most usual ways to interact with real estate professionals. Real estate professionals will contact you after you have placed your home on the market. They usually try to get you to sign a listing with the agency that they represent. You can deal most effectively with them if you understand terms they use.

Agent

An *agent* is a person authorized by another—the *principal*—to act for the principal in dealings with third parties. An agent has certain duties to the principal resulting from the trust relationship, including always acting with the principal's consent, betraying no confidential information, making no secret profit, using reasonable skill and care in performing duties, obeying all lawful instructions, disclosing any material facts (facts that if known would influence a person's decision), and providing an accounting of all money received and disbursed.

You are responsible for the actions of any person you employ as an agent, just as real estate brokers are responsible for the sales associates they employ.

Real Estate Broker

A *broker* is a real estate agent who represents another person in dealing with third parties. To become a broker, a person must take required courses, pass a broker's exam, and be licensed by the state. The broker may employ sales associates, including real estate sales agents and other brokers. The broker is responsible for their actions.

Sales Associate

A *sales* associate is a real estate professional, with either a broker's or salesperson's license, who acts as an agent for a broker.

Single Agent

A *single agent* is an agent representing only one party in a real estate transaction. Types of single agents include a listing agent or seller's agent, who represents the seller in a transaction, and the selling agent or buyer's agent, who represents the buyer.

Dual Agent

A broker acting either directly or through a sales associate as the agent for both the seller and the buyer is known as a *dual agent*. With both parties represented by one agent, great potential exists for imagined or actual conflict of interest.

Divided Agency

The action of an agent in representing both parties in a transaction without the knowledge and consent of both parties creates a *divided agency*. A divided agency is illegal.

Termination of Agency

The representation by an agency may be ended (terminated) by various methods, including:

- Expiration of the agency agreement, the most common method.
- Revocation (cancellation) of the agency by the principal, which may not relieve you of paying commission to a broker.
- Death or incapacity of either the principal or the broker, but not the sales associate.
- Destruction of the property.
- Mutual decision by you and the broker to revoke the agency.
- Renunciation of the agency agreement by the broker.

Commission

Commissions legally belong to and must be paid only to brokers, no matter which sales associates in their organizations obtained the listing or made the sale.

Step 4: Use Real Estate Professionals Most Advantageously

The following are options for dealing with real estate professionals who approach you for a listing. The options are in order from what are generally considered to be the least expensive and restrictive options to those considered the most expensive and restrictive. Legally, commissions are negotiable.

Tell Professional You Are Selling Your Home Yourself

Thank the real estate professional politely for his or her interest but firmly decline any involvement with an agency.

ADVANTAGES
- It encourages real estate professionals to stop calling.
- It maintains good relationships.
- You owe no fees.

DISADVANTAGE
- Professional real estate help is not immediately available in case of questions or problems.

Allow Professional to Represent Buyers

Allow a real estate professional to represent the buyers only if the buyers pay the commission. Make it clear you will *not* sign a listing contract or pay a commission.

ADVANTAGES
- You sign no listing contract.
- You pay no real estate commission.
- You have a professional available for aid in some areas. However, remember that the agent represents the buyers.

DISADVANTAGE
- Because the professional is representing the buyer, this person is not the best source for answers.

Pay Professional by the Hour

If you decide to hire a professional to consult with you at an hourly rate, consider:

1. Checking with independent brokers. They are often the best source of referrals to professional real estate consultants.
2. Asking at several real estate offices to get consultants' names.
3. Signing a contract with the consultant to protect you both.

ADVANTAGES
- You pay only for the services you use.
- Costs are commonly far less than the usual commission.
- You have the services of a real estate professional immediately available.

DISADVANTAGES
- You only get the services for which you pay.
- You pay some fees.

Negotiate Listing Contract for Less Than Usual Fee

The listing fee you negotiate with these brokers could be on a flat-fee or commission basis. Some areas have discount brokers who charge less than the usual fee.

Understand *exactly* what you are getting for what price. Some real estate professionals limit the services they provide on reduced commission or flat-fee contracts. Adding services you need to the basic charge might increase your cost of sale to more than the cost of a usual commission.

ADVANTAGES
- You generally pay less than the usual commission.
- You have the services of a professional immediately available to you.

DISADVANTAGES
- You pay some fees.
- You may have to negotiate to get the rate you want.
- You may receive less than the usual degree of service from the professional by choice or by default.

Sign a "Permission-to-Show" Listing

The "permission-to-show" listing contract allows a professional to show your property only to the person or persons named in that contract. It also provides that you will pay the commission you negotiate only if someone on the list purchases your home.

ADVANTAGES
- Your home may sell more quickly than it might otherwise.
- You must pay a commission only if you sell your home to a person listed on the contract.
- If you sell your home through the professional, you have his or her services immediately available.

DISADVANTAGES
- You must pay the commission if you sell your home to a person listed in the contract.
- You have the professional's services during only part of the process (negotiation and closing).

Have a Broker Submit Your Listing to MLS for a Fee

Find a broker to submit information about your house to your local multiple listing service (MLS) for a fee. Some brokers may do this without having you sign a listing agreement. You then pay a commission only to the broker who brings you buyers. You can set the commission at whatever level you desire. Remember, the lower you set the commission, the less likely real estate professionals will be to show your property.

ADVANTAGES
- Information regarding your home reaches more people who can actively help you sell your home.
- You determine the real estate commission.

DISADVANTAGES
- You pay a fee to list your property with an MLS.
- You pay a commission to sell your home.
- Usually only real estate professionals have access to this information.

Sign an Open Listing

You can sign a nonexclusive open listing granting the right to sell agreement with one or more real estate professionals. It provides that if you sell your home yourself, you are not liable to the broker for a commission. If, however, a real estate professional obtains buyers for the property, you must pay the broker the commission you have negotiated.

ADVANTAGES

- You may sell your home yourself and pay no commission.
- You have the services of a real estate professional available during the whole process.
- Your property may be advertised by more than one real estate professional.

DISADVANTAGES

- Most real estate professionals will not concentrate their money, time, and effort on this type of listing.
- You must pay the commission if a professional procures the buyers.

Sign an Exclusive Agency Listing

Under an exclusive agency listing, which you may sign with only one broker, if that agency obtains the buyers you must pay the broker the commission negotiated. If you sell your home yourself, you are not liable to the broker for the commission.

ADVANTAGES

- You may sell your home yourself and pay no commission.
- You have the services of a real estate professional available during the entire period.

DISADVANTAGES

- Many real estate professionals will not concentrate their sales efforts on this type of listing.
- You must pay the commission you have negotiated if the professional finds the buyers.

Sign an Exclusive Right to Sell Listing

A restricted listing called an exclusive right to sell listing provides that, during the specified term, the broker has the sole and exclusive right to sell your home. It also provides that you must pay the real estate broker the negotiated commission, no matter who makes the sale.

ADVANTAGES

- A real estate professional is most likely to spend the most money, time, and effort on this listing.
- You have the services of a real estate professional during the entire period.

DISADVANTAGE

- You must pay the negotiated commission no matter who sells your home.

Sign a Net Listing

This type of listing provides that the broker retain as commission all money received in excess of the price you set.

ADVANTAGES

- A real estate professional is likely to spend much time, energy, and money on this type of listing.
- You have the services of a real estate professional during the entire period.

DISADVANTAGES

- You may receive far less for your property if you sign this type of listing than if you sign any other.
- Chances of fraud, misrepresentation, and other abuses are more common with this type of listing because of the inexact nature of the commission structure.

Now that you understand what real estate professionals are able to do for you, you can choose to interact with them in a manner that best satisfies your needs.

After you have selected your mix of consultants and have asked them some specific questions about your real estate concerns, you are ready to make a real estate disclosure statement concerning your property. This is the material covered in Chapter 5, "Disclose!"

5

Disclose!

As protection for real estate buyers, laws in some states require sellers to make known things that were previously unknown and that might not be evident. Wherever you live, you can protect yourself by making complete and accurate disclosures.

Step 1: Understand Your Disclosure Responsibilities

Ask closing or escrow personnel, your real estate attorney, or any real estate attorney licensed in your state whether a real estate disclosure statement is required by law on home sales in your state. Laws usually require disclosure for real property improved with specified numbers of dwelling units, often one to four units.

Who?

If your state has a real estate disclosure statement law, chances are you will have to disclose. Ask about the exceptions that apply in your state. The most common exceptions include:

- Transfers from one co-owner to one or more other co-owners.
- Transfers to a spouse or to a direct blood relative.
- Transfers between spouses in connection with a dissolution of marriage or similar proceeding.
- Transfers by a fiduciary (person holding a position of trust) while administering a decedent's (deceased person's) estate, guardianship, conservatorship, or trust.

What?

For a real estate disclosure statement to be valid, laws usually require you to disclose:

1. Information that you know about the property.
2. Information that you, a reasonable homeowner, would be able to find out about the property by making a proper effort.
3. A fair approximation based on the best information available to you listed as such. *If* you don't know *and* you can't find out by making a reasonable effort, state that you are making an approximation. Intentionally or carelessly made errors or omissions can create problems because they can:
   - Be used as a defense if and when buyers refuse to carry out their contractual obligations to buy your home.
   - Be the basis for buyers' action to cancel the contract.
   - Make you liable to the buyers' court action for damages.

How?

You may obtain all information for the disclosure yourself. Consider having a licensed home inspector conduct a physical inspection. A physical inspection is a good source of thorough information of areas covered in real estate disclosure statements. A physical inspection is usually the most cost-effective way to obtain facts about your home's structural integrity. Providing a report as part of your disclosure usually limits your liability.

When you hire an inspector, consider:

1. Hiring an inspector who:
   - Is a trained general contractor, engineer, or architect.
   - Is licensed by a home inspection trade organization.
   - Is knowledgeable about local properties and problems.
   - Has no vested interest in the property, including being someone you would hire to repair any defects.
2. Requiring the inspector to provide you with a detailed written report. Ask the inspector to include items that:
   - Are in good condition.
   - Need repair or replacement.
   - Are not currently problems but may need repair or replacement in the next few years—for example, a roof.

When?

Time your transfer disclosure so that you meet any legal requirements and protect yourself further.

Legal Requirements

To legally protect yourself, consider:

1. Delivery of a detailed disclosure statement about the property as soon as possible before the transfer of title.
2. The law that buyers may cancel within the periods of time specified by your state if you deliver the disclosure after signing a purchase offer. In California, for example, buyers may cancel within three days after personal delivery or five days after the postmarked date, if you mail the statement.

Recommendations

To protect yourself and avoid the time and expense of tying up your property with buyers who do not want the property in its present condition, consider:

1. Preparing a transfer disclosure type statement *before* you put your home on the market.
2. Giving a copy of this disclosure to any prospective buyers who express a serious interest in your property.
3. Having any prospective buyers to whom you give a disclosure sign a written form acknowledging receipt of the disclosure.

Step 2: Prepare Your Disclosure Statement

If you discover that your state requires that you as the seller provide the buyer a real estate disclosure statement, then we suggest you see the Real Estate Disclosure Statement in Section VI, "Worksheets and Contracts." Even if your state mandates a particular real estate disclosure statement, we recommend you still prepare the disclosure statement in Section VI. You can use it as a sample to show to prospective buyers. Then you can obtain and prepare or get help in preparing the state-mandated disclosure statement at a later date. Remember that it is better to let buyers know as much as possible about your property up front, even if the information is negative. In the age of consumerism, *caveat emptor*—let the buyer beware—is dead. You will find it much easier to overcome a buyer's objection at the beginning of a transaction than somewhere in the middle or beyond.

SECTION II

Market

6

Prepare Your Property

Marketing your home includes several related activities, including preparing your home for sale, advertising, and showing your home. How you carry out these activities can influence how quickly your home sells and for what price.

Start marketing by preparing your home to be shown for sale. Homes that have well-thought-out improvements, are in good repair, and are attractive are generally easiest to sell. The sections of this chapter regarding improvements, repairs, and attractiveness each contain information and an accompanying worksheet in Section VI, "Worksheets and Contracts," to aid you in deciding what to do and how to go about doing it.

Step 1: Make Necessary Improvements

The improvements you make to your home generally add to its value, if the remodeling is well done and not an overimprovement. The percentage by which the improvement adds to the value of your home depends on the nature of the improvement and your location. Some improvements are considered more desirable than others, depending on the area of the country, the city, and even the neighborhood in which you live.

Improvements

If you have not made or do not plan to make any improvements, you may want to proceed directly to Step 2, regarding repairs. If you are considering making an improvement, be aware that almost any remodeling will cost more and take longer than you estimate. Most renovations will probably also be less cost-effective than you estimate.

The following list is intended to give you a general idea of the cost-effectiveness of various renovations. The listed improvements are in descending order, with the remodeling generally yielding the greatest percentage of return listed first and those usually yielding the least listed last. Because the same improvement may be considered more desirable in one geographical area than in another, we do not quote specific percentages or ranges. Check with local contractors or building associations for the order and approximate percentage of value added in your area.

Kitchen	Updates and enlargements are usually most cost-effective, overimprovement is not.
Bathrooms	Updates or additions are generally most cost-effective; again, overimprovement is not.
Landscaping	A moderate amount of neat-appearing landscaping is usually cost-effective. Large amounts of landscaping may not be cost-effective because of the amount of maintenance work they represent to many buyers.
Carpeting	Generally most cost-effective if you choose carpet of moderate quality in a neutral color and pattern.
Family Rooms	A location in main living area without reducing other valuable space, such as a garage, is usually best.
Energy-Saving Equipment	Storm windows are most cost-effective in areas where they substantially reduce heating and cooling costs. Roof and attic fans are most cost-effective in warm and hot areas. Storm doors are usually not cost-effective.
Bedrooms	A well-located extra bedroom in a two- or three-bedroom home is generally most cost-effective. Extra bedrooms in larger homes may even decrease the salability.
Central Air Conditioning	Central air is most cost-effective in areas with warm summers and only then where extra ducting need not be installed.
Garages and Carports	Garages are usually more cost-effective in colder climates, near the coast, and in more expensive homes. Carports are usually more cost-effective in warmer areas and less expensive homes.
Wallpaper	Usually most cost-effective if of moderate quality in neutral colors and patterns.
Swimming Pools	Can be somewhat cost-effective in warm or expensive areas. Many buyers do not like the trouble and cost of maintenance or the possible hazard of a pool.
Garage Conversions	Creating a room from a garage is usually not very cost-effective because the conversion makes the house

appear strange from the exterior, and the room is often poorly located in relation to the rest of the house.

Completing the Capital Improvements Worksheet

Use the Capital Improvements Worksheet included in Section VI, "Worksheets and Contracts," to make an inventory of improvements you made on your home. Items on the list have previously been considered tax deductible. Consider:

- Making improvements only if necessary *and* cost-effective.
- Reading the information concerning capital improvements later in this chapter before you decide what projects to undertake.
- Checking with your accountant or tax preparer for the current tax status of these improvements.

Step 2: Perform Repairs That Sell Your Home

Repairing obvious problems generally makes your property sellable to a greater number of buyers. If your home has obvious damage that needs repair *and* you are able to fix it at a reasonable cost, repairs are usually very cost-effective.

Repairs

Do not attempt to conceal problems by making poor or cosmetic repairs. You may be required to make extensive disclosures to buyers regarding your property. Intentionally or carelessly made errors or omissions in the disclosure may leave you liable to buyers for actual damages. The information your state may require you to disclose includes:

- Facts that you know about the property.
- Details you, as a reasonable homeowner, should know about the property.
- A reasonable approximation of facts based on the best information available to you, listed as such (if you do not know and cannot find out by making a reasonable effort).

If you do not contemplate making repairs, proceed directly to Step 3, regarding attractiveness. If you plan to hire professional help in making repairs, consider reading Step 4, regarding contracting, before you choose a contractor.

Completing the Repairs Worksheet

Use the Repairs Worksheet in Section VI, "Worksheets and Contracts," to help you restore your property to a sound condition by:

1. Taking the worksheet to each area mentioned and checking off only those areas that you feel need repair work.
2. Reading the completed list and deciding who will be responsible for ensuring that each task is accomplished.
3. Indicating beside each task the date by which you want the repair accomplished.
4. Indicating beside each task whom you need to contact for the repair and his or her telephone number. If you are repairing the item yourself, indicate the materials you need.
5. Indicating a cost estimate for the repair.
6. Checking off each item as it is completed in the Did column.

Step 3: Enhance Your Home's Attractiveness

Most projects you do to enhance your home's attractiveness are like frosting on a cake. Remember, however, that attractiveness is in the eyes, nose, and ears of the beholder.

Completing the Attractiveness Worksheet

Use the Attractiveness Worksheet in Section VI, "Worksheets and Contracts," to ensure that you handle items that enhance your property's appeal to potential buyers by:

1. Taking the worksheet to each area mentioned and checking off only those items you feel need cosmetic work.
2. Reading the completed list and deciding which member of the household is responsible for seeing that each item is accomplished.
3. Indicating by each item by what date you feel it should be completed.
4. Indicating beside each item whom you need to contact and the company's telephone number or the materials you need if you will do the job yourself.
5. Indicating an estimate, as you obtain it, of how much you expect each item to cost.
6. Checking off each item in the Did column as it is completed.

Step 4: Understand Contracting Out Work

If you have a contractor perform work on your home, consider taking actions to reduce the number of problems you have and to save you time and money. Such preventive actions include:

1. Learning about the work to be done. The more you know about any job, the better your chances are of getting a job done well.

2. Asking for recommendations. Ask others to recommend someone they know does good work or, preferably, someone who did similar work for them satisfactorily, including:
   - Friends, neighbors, and relatives who own property.
   - Real estate professionals.
   - Contractors who work in related fields.
   - Subcontractors who are not dependent on those contractors for their livelihood.

3. Ask pertinent questions. When you initially contact a contractor, ask:
   - The address of his or her established place of business.
   - What licenses he or she has, including contractor's license and business licenses.
   - Whether he or she is bonded.
   - How long he or she has been in business.
   - References for where you can inspect his or her work.
   - List of subcontractors and suppliers.

4. Obtain at least three estimates from competing contractors. If the estimates vary substantially, get more estimates.

5. Choose your contractor.

6. Prepare the contract. Prepare a specific and detailed written agreement with your contractor, including:
   - Names, addresses, and license numbers.
   - Description of the work. Include sketches, plans, and blueprints, as well as a list of products and materials, including brand names and model numbers.
   - Dates. Include starting date, 20-day notice date, and completion date. The 20-day notice is a clause stating that failure to begin work within 20 days of the stated starting date is a violation of the contract and makes the entire contract null and void at your discretion.
   - Cost.
   - Payment schedule. Include a plan of how much you will pay and when. Consider paying in stages of about 20 percent in each installment at the beginning, the end, and as specified portions of the work are completed.
   - Permits and licenses. List permits and licenses and who takes responsibility for obtaining them.
   - Guarantees.
   - Changes in work. A clause to allow your written request for changes without annulling the entire contract.
   - Cleanup. Contractor is responsible for cleaning all debris and removing all excess materials.
   - Owner's rights and responsibilities.
   - Mechanic's lien laws. Incorporate a statement describing your state's mechanic's lien law.

- Cancellation. Include a clause stating that you have three days after signing the contract in which to cancel it.
- Insurance. Incorporate a statement that the contractor is responsible for worker's compensation and liability insurance for his or her workers, subcontractors, and suppliers.
- Completion bond. Make the statement that the contractor will supply a bond. This bond ensures that if the contractor does not complete the project, an insurance company will pay for the rest of the work to be done.
- Arbitration. Incorporate a clause providing for arbitration in the case of contract disputes.
- Unconditional lien release (waiver of liens). Make the statement that the contractor will provide you with an unconditional lien release after the job is complete and you have made the final payments. With this document the contractor waives and releases all his or her mechanic's lien rights, stop notice rights, notice to withhold rights, bond rights, and any and all claims against your property. Without this release you could end up paying twice for the work.
- Bankruptcy. Include a clause stating that if the contractor goes bankrupt you are not liable for the contractor's debts.

7. Read the contract thoroughly and understand it well before you sign it.
   - Do not sign estimates. Estimates may be worded in a manner that makes them binding contracts.
   - Do not make separate agreements with subcontractors or suppliers without checking with your contractor.

8. Ensure the quality of the work by:
   - Being home as much as possible while the contractor is working.
   - Checking the work as it is done.
   - Informing the contractor of problems with the work immediately and in writing.

9. Obtain a detailed, signed receipt stating the amount paid and what the payment was for each time you pay.

10. Sign the certificate of completion and make the final payment only *after:*
    - Work is finished to your satisfaction and according to the terms of the contract.
    - All subcontractors, suppliers, and workers are paid.

11. Make final payment.

12. Keep a copy of all documents about the work.

After you finish preparing for marketing so you can obtain the most money for your home, you are ready to advertise your home for sale.

7
Advertise!

An advertising adage says that 50 percent of all advertising is effective and 50 percent is ineffective. Unfortunately, no one knows for sure which 50 percent is which!

The most important element in successfully marketing your home is giving it the widest possible exposure. As you read this chapter, decide how best to advertise for most productive exposure. You will pay for advertising whether you purchase advertising space or not, due to such circumstances as:

- Making payments on your home for a longer time.
- Having to spend time, effort, and money to maintain your property in top condition to show to prospective buyers.
- Uncertainty and delays in not being able to plan your move.

Step 1: Understand Advertising Basics

Identify the Target Market

Identify the audience that is likely to be interested in purchasing your property. The following categories of property indicate the buyers who are most likely to purchase your type of property.

Suburban Property
- Smaller homes—First-time buyers, young couples without children or with few children, single or divorced persons, older couples, and retirees.
- Larger homes—Buyers who are trading up, large or growing families, and executives.

- Vacation homes—Executives with families and successful young couples as a vacation home; older persons and retirees as their only home.

Urban Property

- Smaller homes or condominiums—First-time buyers, single or divorced persons, successful young people, and executives for a house in town.
- Larger homes or condominiums—Buyers who are trading up, successful young couples, and corporations for the periodic use of their executives.

Learn about Laws

Understand and comply with laws regarding discrimination and disclosure in advertising.

Discrimination

Discrimination is the arbitrary selection of certain types of persons from a larger group and the giving to or withholding from these persons certain advantages. Treating other persons unfairly and denying them normal privileges are both forms of discrimination. Housing discrimination on the basis of race, color, religion, sex, marital status, national origin, or ancestry is illegal under the federal Civil Rights Act of 1968. Check laws in your area. Laws in many areas prohibit:

- Discriminating on the basis of sexual preference.
- Asking buyers about their race, color, religion, sex, marital status, national origin, ancestry, or sexual preferences.
- Indicating any preferences for or against any such factor.
- Discriminating against anyone who has previously opposed your prior discriminatory procedures.

Disclosure

Disclosure, or making known things that were previously unknown, is also required by federal and state laws. For your own protection:

- State only correct information in your advertising.
- If some items of information you list are estimates, state that they are approximations.
- Understand that if you make intentional or careless errors or omissions, you may be violating disclosure laws.

Understand Types of Advertising

Advertising your home for sale encompasses all forms of attracting attention, including signs, newspapers, newsletters, flyers, bulletin boards, and telling friends and co-workers. Planning for productive handling of telephone inquiries is also part of effective advertising.

Signs

Signs, one of the most productive forms of real estate advertising, usually work best when they suggest quality, care, and concern.

ADVANTAGES

- Signs are relatively inexpensive.
- They let neighbors know you are selling your property.
- They reach people familiar with the neighborhood. (These persons are a good source of referrals, because they like and can afford property in the area.)

DISADVANTAGES

- Even if you have a telephone number and the message "By Appointment Only," people may still ring your doorbell and ask to see your home.
- When signs remain in place for a long period, it becomes obvious that you have not been able to sell your home.

Effective Signs. Productive signs are usually:

- Rectangular in shape and approximately 18 by 24 inches,
- Visible against landscaping or building,
- Simple and easy to read,
- Capable of being read from a car moving in either direction along a street at a normal speed.

Size and Placement. Laws in some cities and restrictions in some subdivisions may limit size and/or placement of signs. Consider:

1. Checking with your city for any applicable laws.
2. Examining a copy of your subdivision covenants, conditions, and restrictions (CC&Rs) for sign regulations.
3. Asking permission of property owners before putting signs on their property. (Requests can keep you on good terms with other residents and allow you to tell them about your home sale.)
4. Placing your signs where they can be safely read while you follow local laws and customs.

Types of Signs. Two types of signs are generally used by owners who sell their homes themselves: for-sale-by-owner signs and open-house signs.

For-sale-by-owner signs say you are selling your home yourself. The preferred wording is *For Sale by Owner,* followed by a blank area on which you can write your telephone number with chalk or marking pen, and then by the words *By Appointment Only.* These signs are easy to read and yet give the necessary information. The requirement for an appointment usually does not discourage serious buyers, but rather prevents the curious from dropping by unexpectedly or at inconvenient times.

Open-house signs let the public know that your home is open for viewing. Area open houses, discussed later in this chapter, require no signs and are more likely to be instrumental in selling your home.

Placement of Signs. The following are tips for placing the for-sale-by-owner signs:

1. Place signs in your yard so that they are visible from both directions from any streets that border your property.
2. Leave these signs in place at all times for maximum effect, except when you will be away for several days or more.
3. Take signs down if you have no one to at least answer calls.

If you decide to hold an open house for the public, you should know about small and large open-house signs. Attach a small open-house sign to the same pole as your large for-sale-by-owner sign when you hold an open house. Consider using a large sign that states simply *Open House* and then has two blank areas to be filled in with chalk or marking pen. Put your street address in the first blank and your telephone number in the second.

To place open-house signs for maximum exposure:

1. Put signs on both corners of your block, preferably on the same side of the street as your home.
2. Place a sign at the nearest major intersection or major street near your home—the closer to your home, the better.

Flags

Use flags to draw attention to your signs. Use flags especially if you must place a sign where it is difficult to see or where it competes with other signs.

Newspapers

The type of advertising you do in a newspaper and type of newspaper you choose depend on the kind of house you have and the effect you desire. Classified and display advertisements are different in effectiveness, rates, and composition.

Classified Advertisements. Classifieds are the easier of the two types to write, cheaper, and function better for most homes.

*   *Effectiveness* of this form of advertising is greatest when you use several small ads stressing different advantages of your home. In this way you reach more types of people than with a single large advertisement.
*   *Rates* for these ads are usually inexpensive. Ask newspapers for their schedule of rates. Note what special rates apply to what

number of insertions and what number of consecutive insertions.

- *Composition* of an ad can make a difference in buyers' responses.
  - Use large, specific headlines and capital letters. Be concise. Use two- to three-word headlines.
  - Describe the property's key features, using words with attractive meanings.
  - Make each advertisement brief but use descriptive *whole* words and phrases. (Abbreviations are often difficult to understand.)
  - Emphasize the benefits your home has for the buyer and that it is an unbeatable value.

			C	O	M	P	L	E	T	E	L	Y		R	E	M	O	D	E	L	E	D	!				
O	p	e	n	,		a	i	r	y	,		l	a	r	g	e		c	o	r	n	e	r		l	o	t	,
h	u	g	e		m	a	s	t	e	r		s	u	i	t	e	,		3	B	R		2	B	A		
$	2	0	0	,	0	0	0		C	a	l	l		O	w	n	e	r		5	5	5	-	2	4	5	5

- Surround the ad with blank (white) space to make it easier to read and stand out from other ads.
- Include information in the approximate order listed here. Change the order to list most attractive features first or to support the headline.
  1. List of best features
  2. Number of bedrooms and baths
  3. Price
  4. Terms
  5. Demand for action ("Phone today for an appointment!")
  6. For sale by owner
  7. Telephone number
- Do not exaggerate.
- Omit your address so that buyers call you to get further information; in this way you can screen callers over the telephone, be ready for buyers when they arrive in order to show your home to best advantage, and discourage theft while you are not at home.

Select the best two or three advertisements and set them aside. Rewrite the best ads after you have set them aside for a period of time, preferably overnight.

Place the advertisement under the appropriate heading in the classified section, usually under *Homes for Sale* in the city or area where your home is located.

If you decide to run an ad for several weeks, consider running at least two versions on alternate weeks. Buyers are less likely to decide something is wrong with your property because it has not sold.

Display Advertisements. Display ads may be effective in special situations.

- *Effectiveness* of these larger advertisements is greatest for immense and unique homes or for special promotions.
- *Rates* are generally expensive, and usually you must pay in advance. Sometimes special rates are offered for a combination of classified and display advertisements.
- *Composition* is similar to that for a classified ad. Explain in more detail about the special features of your property. Newspapers will often help you compose display ads, usually at no charge.
- *Lead times* vary among newspapers. Ask newspaper representatives the length of their lead time, as well as their policies on canceling an ad. Many newspapers have a two- to three-day lead time between placing the order and running the ad. Generally you must pay a penalty or forfeit your whole payment if you cancel during the lead time.

Types of Newspapers. Effectiveness and rates vary depending on the type of newspaper in which you advertise. *General circulation dailies* are usually effective for reaching the most people at the lowest rate per person. *Local dailies* are often especially good for attracting people who want another home in the same area or who are considering moving into a specific area. *Weeklies* are generally not very effective unless they are the only newspaper in a rural area. *Special interest* papers are generally like newsletters. They may be effective if your home has unique features important to persons with similar special interests.

To avoid charges of discrimination, run an ad in a newspaper of general circulation every time you run one for more limited circulation.

Newsletters

Groups with special interests usually receive newsletters.

- *Effectiveness* of newsletters depends on whether your home has unique features important to persons with special interests.
- *Rates* and costs vary, but newsletter ads are usually fairly inexpensive.
- *Composition* of the ad may be handled as for newspapers. Newsletters may have both classified and display advertisements. Check with newsletter staff for specific requirements.
- *Lead times* depend on how often a newsletter is published. Check with newsletter staff for a schedule.

Magazines

Effectiveness, rates, composition, and lead times of real estate advertisements in magazines vary greatly, depending on the nature of the magazine. Inexpensive formats are often published weekly on inexpensive paper. Expensive formats are usually published less often, printed on more expensive paper, and normally contain pictures (sometimes in color).

For magazines devoted to shoppers in general, the most effective are usually those in which the advertisements are classified and you can target your ad to the locality you desire by selecting areas by ZIP code.

- *Effectiveness* of magazines in selling your home varies with the magazine format and the nature of the home. Inexpensive formats of classified ads to make ads easy to locate can be cost-effective for moderately priced homes. Some magazines devoted solely to real estate may allow or require a photograph. If you use a photograph, be sure it compliments your home so that potential buyers will get a good impression. Expensive formats are usually not cost-effective except for unique and expensive homes.
- *Rates* vary by format also. Inexpensive formats have prices that may range from inexpensive to expensive, depending on the publication. Usually they are costlier if a photograph is required. Expensive formats have costs that are quite high. Some magazines require expensive color photographs.
- *Composition* depends on the type of magazine. Check with magazine staff for details. Some publications require photographs processed by special methods.
- *Lead time* varies depending on how often the magazine is published. Check with magazine staff for details.

Flyers

Flyers are leaflets for mass distribution. They should accurately describe your property. They are relatively inexpensive and easily distributed. If information such as your asking price changes, you have to print new flyers. Used indiscriminately, flyers may create litter.

- *Effectiveness* of flyers depends on several factors. Choose the methods that work best for you.
  - Give buyers who have just viewed your property flyers as they leave so that they have information regarding your property. (If you give them flyers before you show them the property, they may not pay full attention during the tour.)
  - Give flyers to neighbors after they have viewed your home when you hold an area open house.
  - Post them on bulletin boards at strategic locations.
  - Mail flyers to the Chamber of Commerce, which often gets inquiries about properties for sale in the area.
- *Composition* of your flyer varies with your locale, the market, and price of the property. Review the sample Home for Sale

Flyer in Section VI, "Worksheets and Contracts," explained here. It lists some of the most commonly used descriptions for relevant sections. In some cases it may be appropriate to list more than one option, for example, Exterior: Brick and frame.

Community: Name of city, town, or area where your property is located.

Nearest major cross streets: Names of major streets that cross nearest to your property to enable a buyer to find your property easily.

Approximate square feet: Number of square feet of living area. Living area usually *excludes* the garage unless garage is finished and converted into a usable room in the house.

Style: Bungalow, Cape Cod, Colonial, Contemporary, Dutch Colonial, French Provincial, Ranch, Spanish, Split Level, Traditional, Tudor, Victorian.

Exterior: Adobe, aluminum siding, block, brick, brick veneer, frame, stone, stucco, wood.

Roof: Composition shingle, concrete shake, gravel, rock, shake, slate, tile, wood shingle.

Age: Approximate age of your home.

Lot size: Approximate square feet of lot size.

Lot character: Corner, cul-de-sac, irregular, pie-shaped, rectangular, square.

View: Bay, canyon, city, golf course, green belt, lagoon, lake, mountains, ocean, panoramic, trees, valley.

Stories: Enter number of stories.

Floors: Carpet, hardwood, metal, slab, vinyl, wood.

Living room, dining room, family room, bedrooms 1–5, and *den:* Approximate square feet.

Extra room: Room purpose (breakfast, library, office, sewing, sitting, storage) and approximate square feet.

Fireplace: Room or rooms that have fireplaces, nature of the fireplace (brick, metal, stone, freestanding), and any amenities (gas starter, gas log).

Garage: Number of vehicles for which garage was constructed and that it can comfortably fit (one, two, three) and the placement (attached or detached). If you have a carport, enter carport in this space and the number of vehicles it can accommodate (one, two, three).

Garage door opener: Yes if you have it on all garage doors or on which door you have the opener, if it is only on one (single, double).

Laundry: Location (garage, inside, room) and utilities available in that area (electric, gas, propane).

Patio: Nature (covered, deck, enclosed, gazebo, porch, screened) and construction (brick, concrete, flagstone, wood).

Pool: Nature (above ground, gunite, vinyl liner). If heated, enter heated and source of heat (diesel, electric, gas, propane, solar). If unheated, enter unheated.

Spa: Nature (above ground, gunite, hot tub, Jacuzzi). If heated, enter heated and source of heat (diesel, electric, gas, propane, solar). If unheated, enter unheated.

Sauna: Location.

Television: Nature of reception equipment (antenna, cable, dish).

Fence: Nature of fence (brick wall, cinder block, chain link, split rail, stock, wood, wrought iron) and coverage (front, rear, side, total).

Sewer: Nature of system (seepage pit, septic tank, sewer) and conditions it meets (available, approved, bond, needs percolation test, paid for).

Water: Source (public, private, well) and any modifying factors (filtered, softener).

Sprinklers: If present, location (front, partial, rear, total).

Water heater: Source of heat (electric, gas, propane, solar).

Heating: Type and nature (baseboard, floor, forced air [electric, gas, propane], heat pump, radiant [electric, fluid], solar, wall [electric, gas]).

Air conditioning: Nature (evaporative cooler, forced air [electric, gas], heat pump) and location (central, window).

Stove: Source of heat (electric, gas, propane).

Oven: Number of ovens (single, double) and nature (electric, gas, propane, self-cleaning).

Microwave: Pertinent information (built-in, not included).

Smoke detector: Number (one, two) and type (battery, electric).

Dishwasher: Pertinent information (built-in, not included).

Disposal: Yes if there is one, no if there is not.

Trash compactor: Pertinent information (built-in, not included).

Price: Amount you are asking for your property.

Financing: First loan (mortgage or trust deed) and/or second loan.

Payment: Payment amount and period to which it applies.

Lender: Name of the organization or person who made the loan.

Due date: When the loan balance is payable.

Take over: Yes if loan can be taken over by buyers; no if not.

Interest %: Percentage rate. If variable, so note.

Possession date: Date that buyers may take possession.

[ ] Planned development [ ] Condominium: Check if appropriate.

Homeowner's fees, maintenance, water, trash, insurance: Amounts, if applicable.

Recreation room, pool, spa: Yes if present; no if not.

Tennis: Yes and number of courts if present; no if not.

Golf: Yes and number of holes if present; no if not.

Schools: Names of nearest schools in whose district your property is located.

Notes: Items that have not been covered before or that you wish to describe in greater detail.

Bulletin Boards

Bulletin boards in locations frequented by people you think might be interested in purchasing your property are good places to post flyers. Such areas could include local community centers, athletic clubs, social clubs, churches, colleges and universities, and the clubhouse of a planned unit development. Be sure to get permission from whoever is in charge before posting your flyer at any of these sites.

Using flyers on bulletin boards is a relatively inexpensive form of advertisement. Getting permission from the proper authority before posting a flyer on the bulletin board can be time-consuming, however.

Co-workers, Friends, and Neighbors

Let your co-workers, friends, and neighbors know that your home is for sale.

1. Encourage people to tell others about your home.
2. Give acquaintances flyers describing your property.
3. Invite acquaintances to your area open house.

Open Houses

Inviting your neighbors to view your open house is more effective than a public open house and is also safer.

Area Open House. Neighbors usually already know that your home is for sale. They are more likely to recommend your home to others after they see what your property has to offer. If you decide to hold an area open house, consider:

1. Preparing your area open-house announcement indicating you:
   a. Are inviting your neighbors to an area open house to view your property, which is for sale.
   b. Will be serving refreshments during the open house.
2. Making enough copies to distribute these invitations for several blocks around your property.
3. Distributing invitations to the houses you choose.
4. Having the viewers sign a guest register as they enter.

Public Open House. Public open houses often attract many people who are not serious buyers or cannot afford your property. Real estate professionals generally hold public open houses primarily to gain potential clients. They seldom sell a property as the result of a public open house.

Multiple Listing Service (MLS)

The MLS is a service to which real estate brokers belong in order to share their listings and commissions with fellow members of the service. As of this writing, only real estate brokers may make submissions to the MLS. Some brokers will submit your home to an MLS for a nominal fee.

See Chapter 4, "Select Your Consultants," for more details about how to maximize the benefits real estate professionals can offer as you sell your property yourself, as well as other possible interactions you may have with real estate professionals.

Internet

The Internet can provide a wonderful vehicle for selling your home, *if* you know how to use it effectively. There are several advantages to using the Internet for selling your home.

1. The costs for showing your home are generally quite inexpensive.
2. You are able to show in pictures the advantages of your home without anyone actually disturbing you.
3. There is a wider potential audience for the sale of your home.

If you know little about setting up a Web site or are planning to use the Internet as your primary means of advertising, we suggest you consider using a service or services. Their prices are generally quite inexpensive for the service they provide—starting at free. There are many services located all over the world, so check out the services they have to offer before you decide. To locate the sites, log on to the Internet and use a search engine such as Metacrawler, Profusion, Northern Light, Excite, AltaVista, or Yahoo! and type in "For Sale By Owner." You will come up with many sites. You might also check the list of for sale by owner sites by the *International Real Estate Digest* at www.ired.com/dir/fsbo.htm.

Whether you set up your own Web site or use a service, having your home on the Internet works well in conjunction with other methods of advertising. If you are using some other method(s) than the Internet to market your home, we suggest you put the Internet address where you put any other sales information. This includes on signs, flyers, and bulletin boards and in ads in newspapers, magazines, and newsletters. Also give the information to co-workers, friends, and neighbors, so that they may let others know about your home for sale. Potential buyers can get a better idea if they are actually interested before they contact you.

There are several aspects to setting up and getting information about your home on the Internet: gathering the information, taking the pictures, editing the pictures, and setting up the Web page. You can set up your own Web page, or pay someone or a service to set up your Web page for you.

Gathering the Information. The information you gather for a home for sale flyer is the most important information you need for selling your home on the Internet. You may add a few more details if you choose. However, we suggest that you keep it short.

Pictures. Prepare your property for taking pictures. Remember with pictures there are only a few images from which buyers will get an impression of your property, so make those images work for you. Do the things we suggest in previous chapters of this book.

- Make all the necessary improvements.
- Perform repairs that sell your home.
- Enhance you home's attractiveness.
- Make the appropriate finishing touches.
- Above all make the area neat before you take the picture. Put away as many possessions as you can to make your home look neat without making the area look vacant for several reasons:
  ° It allows the features of the home itself to assume more importance. You are not selling your possessions, you are selling your home.
  ° Not everyone has the same taste in possessions. Some people dislike an item you might consider a prized possession. You want buyers to imagine how their possessions would look in the home you are selling.
  ° With pictures of your possessions on the Internet for everyone to see you may encourage burglars.
- You may not even notice items that to others may detract from the picture. Such often overlooked items include vehicles (automobiles, trucks, vans, RV's, etc.); hoses for watering and those attached to automatic pool cleaners; pets; and children's toys.
- Taking the pictures:
  ° Light the area to show the features of your home and to make it look more appealing.
  ° Take a picture at a time of day where the area looks its best.
  ° Illuminate the area with lights if it is naturally dark. Your eye can adjust to many levels of light. Your camera may not.
  ° Remember, even an automatic camera does not see things the way your eye does.
- Take the picture at angles that are most complimentary to your home.

The pictures to take will depend on where you live.

- For single-family homes:
  ° Front of house, including the front yard.
  ° Living room, including unique features such as fireplace.
  ° Kitchen.

- ° Den, family room, dining room, or any area that has noteworthy features, such as built-ins, paneling, etc.
  - ° Bathroom if it has noteworthy fixtures or features.
  - ° View if a major selling feature.
  - ° Backyard, including decks or pool if present.
- For planned unit developments, pictures of common areas may be important to some potential buyers. Remember though that the people must live *in* the home, so most will want to see more pictures of the home itself.
- Entry into development.
- Recreation facilities.
- Greenbelts.

Still pictures are preferred by most people. They download relatively quickly and take no additional software to view. The equipment to take them is readily available and relatively inexpensive. Stills can be more easily and inexpensively edited to show exactly what is wanted.

Having videos gives the potential buyer more of a sensation of actually seeing your home in person. Unfortunately, videos take more time to download because they are basically a series of still pictures. Buyers may get tired of waiting and go to another site if yours takes too long. You need specific software to run the video. Although the software is usually available for free, if the potential buyer does not have the software, the buyer must download the software. This process takes time, at best and may lead them away from your site to which they never return, at worst. If you use video, we suggest using short segments of the most important features only to keep download times to a minimum.

Once pictures are in digital format, they can be easily transferred to and worked with most computers.

- Still pictures on film:
  - ° Pictures on film must be developed by some process, some of which require that you take the film to a processor to be developed.
  - ° Some processors provide the pictures digitally on a floppy disk or a CD-ROM so that they may be easily transferred to your computer. It may be worth it and cost effective to you to find a processor who provides this service.
  - ° Using a scanner, scan the pictures or find someone to scan it for you to get the picture in a digital format.
- Digital still pictures:
  - ° Digital still cameras take pictures in a format that may easily be transferred to your computer.
  - ° Digital video cameras often have a method of getting still shots. Digital pictures can be easily transferred to most computers, where they can be worked on with photo editing programs.

- Additional equipment and programs are needed to edit and process the video for the Internet. Most common video cameras (VHS and SVHS, 8 and High-8) have a poorer quality image than digital cameras. Also, the image they take must be digitized by the additional equipment. The equipment and programs are generally more expensive than still equipment.
- Image editing programs for stills—computer programs are available that allow you to prepare the pictures for showing on the Internet. You may want to have a program that does the items listed below or hire someone who has the ability to manipulate the digital image in these ways:
  - ° Crop or cut off the picture to eliminate areas you do not want to show.
  - ° Lighten the picture if it is too dark or darken a too light picture.
  - ° Erase the image of something you do not want to be seen, such as a hose your forgot to remove before taking the picture. The process can be time-consuming if you do it yourself and expensive if someone else does it. It is usually easier to be careful when you take your shots in the first place. We do not suggest erasing any structural item.
  - ° Sharpen the picture. Sharpening makes the edges of an object more defined.
- Image editing equipment for videos. While some of the image editing capabilities available for stills are also available for videos, a similar manipulation of video is very expensive because every frame must be altered individually.

Picture considerations.

- Format. The formats .jpg and .gif are most universally accepted for Internet use because they take up less room for the same picture than some other formats. They can also be read widely by Web browsers. Use .jpg files for photographs and .gif files for line art, such as floor plans.
- Quality. The standard is 72 dpi (dots per inch), which is the most most computer monitors are capable of. Though with other pictures, the more dpi the better the quality of the picture, on the Internet this just creates a larger picture.
- Size. The larger the picture the more memory it uses. The amount of area a picture will take up on a buyer's computer monitor's screen depends on the size of the monitor and the resolution the video card is set for. It is suggested that no picture be larger than 600 pixels wide. If text is desired beside the picture then a size not greater then 400 pixels wide is often recommended.

Number and Order of Pictures.

- One picture of each area.
  - A picture may show a bit of another area to show its relationship to the other areas.
  - Many pictures of the same area and none of the others may cause a buyer to wonder what the problem is with the other areas.
- Put the pictures in the order you would show them to someone to whom you were giving a tour of your house. That order is usually something like:
  - Front of house.
  - Living room.
  - Kitchen.
  - Den, family room, or other noteworthy area.
  - Back yard.
  - Show a view after the picture of the area from whatever area is best.

Listing on Search Engines. If you are using the Internet as the primary way to advertise your home for sale being listed on search engines may be very important to you. Getting listed on search engines takes time and know-how. Different search engines index on different criteria and take different amounts of time to index the information. You can pay services to send your information to a variety of search engines, but be sure they use the proper criteria for each service, and not just sending out all the information in one format.

Most services are already listed on a variety of search engines, so there is no lag time in people locating the site where your property is listed. Ask the services what search engines they are listed on. More is usually better in this case because that means more ways for potential buyers to find your information and hopefully a quicker sale.

Step 2: Plan Your Advertising Budget

Plan and keep in mind how much you are willing to spend on advertising.

Advertising Budget Information

As a basic budget for selling your home yourself, consider the following:

- For-sale-by-owner signs at a one-time cost of $50 to $100.
- Classified advertisements in local papers at approximately $100 per week.
- Flyers at $100 to $300, depending on the nature and number required.

Completing the Advertising Budget Worksheet

Prepare an advertising budget for the sale of your home on the Advertising Budget Worksheet in Section VI, "Worksheets and Contracts."

Step 3: Prepare Telephone Response

Because the more calls you receive the greater chance you have of selling your property, consider:

- Remaining at the telephone number you list on your advertisements as much as possible.
- Listing a time (for example, evenings) and a telephone number when and where you can be reached, if you are not available the whole day.
- Asking your employer before listing your work number on advertisements.

Telephone Register

A telephone register is a listing of information regarding telephone calls you receive.

Understand Use of Telephone Register

A telephone register, which you fill out during each call, can be a valuable source of information regarding:

- The advertising method that triggered each call, which helps you determine the most effective methods.
- Who called and his or her telephone number, which allows you to get in touch with callers again, if necessary.
- With whom and for when you made appointments.
- Callers' remarks, which may be helpful in addressing callers' interests and concerns when you show them your home.

Prepare Telephone Register

Consider using the Telephone Register in Section VI, "Worksheets and Contracts," in conjunction with the suggested telephone screening conversation by:

1. Copying several Telephone Register sheets.
2. Placing the sheets in a binder or folder.
3. Keeping the binder or folder near the telephone.
4. Entering the pertinent information as you are speaking to each prospective buyer.

Telephone Screening Conversation

To obtain necessary information from potential buyers without over-selling your home, consider using a conversation similar to the one described here. Remember, your goal is to make an appointment with buyers to show your property.

In Person

See Section VI, "Worksheets and Contracts," for a blank worksheet. Manage the in-person telephone conversation as follows:

1. Speak the wording given on the left side of the page.
2. Do not speak the words in parentheses ( ). They are for your information only.
3. Allow the caller time to respond before continuing with the next remark or question.
4. Write information received in the Telephone Register.

By Answering Machine or Voice Mail

Although using an answering machine or voice mail is less preferable than responding to the telephone in person, an answering machine or voice mail is still a very effective tool in marketing your property. (Section VI, "Worksheets and Contracts," for a blank worksheet.) It allows you to be away from home and still receive calls from prospective buyers, as well as screen your calls. See Section VI, "Worksheets and Contracts," for a blank worksheet for composing your answering machine or voice mail message.

Step 4: Implement Your Advertising Plans

Put your advertising plans into action, now that you understand advertising basics, have planned your budget, and have prepared your telephone response.

The response to your advertising depends on local market conditions, pricing your home correctly, and the scope of your advertising. Repetition is the key to successful advertising. Plan on a minimum 30-day advertising campaign. It only takes one buyer seeing your ads to successfully sell your home yourself.

After you implement your advertising plans you are ready to take the steps necessary to show your home to prospective buyers.

8

Show Your Home Successfully

Showing your home successfully includes safeguarding your property, protecting viewers, making finishing touches, managing the home tour, selling your home, and completing the sale.

Step 1: Safeguard Your Property

Take steps to protect your property and yourself. Consider these precautions:

1. Hiding valuables.
   - Hide anything that might be broken or easily taken.
   - Conceal large valuables, such as fine china, silver, pieces of art, and other prized possessions.
   - Avoid mentioning what valuables you have. Persons looking for a home to buy will not be interested.
2. Have all viewers sign the guest register and show picture identification, such as a driver's license:
   - Gives you the viewer's name, address, and telephone number so that you may make follow-up contact.
   - Shows the effectiveness of your advertising:
     - Inquire of each person who views your home specifically where he or she learned about your house.
     - Tally the number of persons learning about your home from each source.
   - Discourages a would-be thief.
3. Accompany anyone viewing your home.
   - Make appointments to show your home.

- Have family or friends aid you during an open house. Tell them to ask buyers who arrive while you are showing your home to wait for the next tour.
- Have everyone enter and leave by one door to control the flow of traffic.
- Invite buyers who return to view your home for a second time to view it unaccompanied:
  - Buyers are not inhibited by your presence.
  - Buyers have freedom to explore your home and study how your property would fit their needs.
  - You stay in one room or step outside.
  - You remain in the area so you are available to answer questions buyers may have.
4. Decline to discuss your lifestyle or schedule with viewers. People really interested in buying your home will not be interested in your personal affairs.

Step 2: Protect Viewers

Protect your viewers from possible injury and yourself from possible lawsuits.

1. Make walking safe by:
   - Putting down rubber mats or other nonslip surfacing on slick areas.
   - Tacking down mats or throw rugs that might slip.
   - Putting away items over which viewers might trip.
2. Lock up anything potentially dangerous that children might discover, including:
   - Household chemicals, such as cleaning compounds, medicines, toiletries, painting supplies, and gardening chemicals.
   - Dangerous instruments, such as guns and knives.
3. Childproof your yard, including decks, patios, pools, spas, and hot tubs.
4. Secure pets, even ones that have always been friendly. Lock them in an enclosure if they are usually quiet, or arrange for them to stay with a neighbor or in a kennel if they are likely to be noisy.
5. Arrange with a neighbor to accompany you or keep an eye out if you feel uneasy showing your home to a man or a couple.

Step 3: Make Finishing Touches

Finishing touches can make a difference when you sell your home. They convey to buyers the idea that you care about the home and find it a wonderful place to live.

If you used the Repair Worksheet and Attractiveness Worksheet, all you need to show your home to best advantage are the finishing touches, which you can review on the Finishing Touches Checklist in Section VI, "Worksheets and Contracts."

1. Look successful. When people shop for property, they also shop for lifestyle. Usually wearing tasteful, casual attire is most appropriate.
2. Make sure property is orderly.
3. Make walking safe. Put away anything viewers might trip over or slip on.
4. Secure pets.
5. Arrange for children to be away or stay with neighbors or friends while you show your home.
6. Create quiet or pleasing sounds. Turn off all appliances, as well as radio, television, and stereo except for possible soft background music.
7. Make sure that the air temperature is in a pleasant range.
8. Turn on lights.
9. Open window coverings, such as drapes, curtains, or shades.
10. Display the benefits of your property, as appropriate. Light the fireplace if it is cold outside or turn on air conditioning if it is hot outside.
11. Create pleasing visual images. Use such items as vases of flowers, a bowl of fruit, and reading material that might interest typical buyers of your home.
12. Create pleasing smells.
    - Refrain from cooking strong-smelling food before showing your home.
    - Eliminate smoke odor with activated charcoal placed in inconspicuous areas.
    - Be sure that pet areas are clean.
    - Bake bread or cookies or brew a pot of coffee.
    - Put a drop of vanilla on foil in a warm oven.
    - Simmer water and citrus peels with such spices as allspice, nutmeg, and cinnamon.
13. Check bathrooms for tidiness just before viewers arrive. Close the toilet lid.

Step 4: Manage Home Tour

To manage the home tour to show your home to its best advantage, consider:

1. Planning the tour to emphasize the best features of your home. Show the best features at the beginning or end of the tour.

2. Having viewers sign a guest register. Copy the Guest Register in Section IV, "Worksheets and Contracts," and put the copies in a notebook for viewers to sign.

3. Accompanying viewers at all times, remembering to:
   - Give viewers adequate time to see your home.
   - Stay with viewers and guide them to the strong points, but do not hover.
   - Refrain from intruding in conversations viewers have among themselves.
   - Listen carefully and with sincere interest.
   - Ask only a few questions. Do not pry.

4. Refrain from negotiating during the tour. You can bargain more effectively later.

Step 5: Sell Your Home

While you are showing prospective buyers your property, you may be more effective if you use low-key sales techniques. Read the methods listed here several times but don't try to memorize them.

1. Know the area. Be able to talk intelligently with buyers about such items as:
   - Climate, terrain, and environmental hazards.
   - Age distribution in neighborhood and town planning.
   - Schools, including location and quality.
   - Services and utilities.
   - Recreation facilities and neighborhood improvements.
   - Traffic, transportation, parking, and noise levels.
   - Tax base, zoning, and assessments.
   - Crime rate in the area, plus police and fire protection.
   - Health care facilities and hospitals.
   - Churches and other places of worship.

2. Know your property. It gives you credibility and inspires buyers' confidence. Be able to talk intelligently about:
   - Brand names and capacities of major systems and appliances.
   - Insulation, including ceilings, walls, and windows.
   - Utility costs and property taxes.

3. Be polite and friendly in a reserved manner.
   - Be relaxed and confident to give buyers confidence in you and in themselves.
   - Avoid an argument with the viewers. You may win the argument and lose the sale.

4. Answer all questions honestly, briefly, and confidently.
   - Do not exaggerate.

- If you are selling because of some distress situation (divorce, job loss, illness), keep your reasons for selling to yourself. This way, they cannot be used against you in the negotiation process.

5. If you do not know the answer to a question, tell buyers that you don't know. Inform buyers that you will be happy to find out the answer and tell them. Then be sure to do so.

6. Appeal to buyers' needs.
   - Let most of the outstanding features that meet the buyers' needs speak for themselves.
   - Sell the benefits as a way of life for the buyer (not the features) in a brief manner. Do not oversell.

7. Handle buyers' objections.
   - Objections may be a sign that buyers are seriously interested in your home.
   - Try to understand buyers' objections by putting yourself in the buyers' place.
   - After empathizing with viewers:
     ◦ Agree briefly that the objection is valid. Tell how you handled it so it was not a disadvantage.
     ◦ You can also acknowledge that the objection is valid, then explain why it is minor compared to the other qualities of your home.
     ◦ A third alternative is to agree by nodding your head, then change the subject, if the objection depends on personal taste or if you found no way to surmount it.

8. Consider inviting buyers who are viewing your home for the second time to do so unaccompanied by you. Unaccompanied buyers have freedom to explore your home to study how your property would fit their needs. Stay in one room or step outside. You stay in the area so you are available to answer any questions buyers may have.

Step 6: Complete the Sale

Restating the good points of your home is of no use if viewers are already interested in buying it. When viewers make statements that sound as if they might be seriously interested in purchasing your home, *stop selling and start completing the sale!*

1. Ask buyers whether they are interested in submitting an offer.
2. Ask buyers when you can schedule an appointment for them to present an offer to you.
3. Request that buyers submit an offer to you that is in writing, covers all important issues, and is accompanied by a personal

or cashier's check made out to an acceptable closing or escrow agent.

4. Ask buyers if the company or person you would like to use for the closing is acceptable to them.

5. Give buyers a copy of appropriate documents you prepared:
   - A copy of your disclosure statement.
   - Copies of all inspection reports issued in the last two years concerning the condition of your home.

6. Request that buyers contact a lender and be prequalified for a home loan. Explain that:
   - Buyers' prequalification aids in making a decision regarding the offer, if buyers do not have all cash.
   - A lender can issue a written guarantee to finance buyers' home purchase in a specified price range, at a certain interest rate (or within a range), and for a specified time.
   - A lender can issue a written guarantee for a short-term bridge or gap loan to buyers who are simultaneously selling one house and trying to buy another.

7. Ask whether buyers feel comfortable preparing an offer. If not, you might:
   - Give buyers a copy of the purchase contract to read.
   - Suggest that buyers write down on a separate sheet of paper the way they intend to fill out the form.
   - Suggest that you will write the offer with the buyers when you get together the next time.

8. Read the section of Chapter 9 dealing with reevaluating your goals *before* you set up an appointment to negotiate the sale of your property.

9. Read all of Section III of this book before you start to negotiate.

10. When you get an offer:
    - Proceed to read Section III of this book.
    - Continue to show your property until you have made an agreement. This agreement should include a signed offer and a check.

Now that you have shown your home successfully, you are ready to prepare for negotiation. Preparing for negotiation includes reevaluating your goals, preparing a preliminary estimate of proceeds, setting up the offer presentation, managing the offer presentation, and being aware of the possibility of revocation of the offer.

SECTION III
Negotiate

9

Prepare for Negotiation

Prepare for negotiation by reevaluating your goals, scheduling an offer presentation, managing the offer presentation, and being aware of the possibility of a revocation of the offer by buyers.

Step 1: Reevaluate Your Goals

Reevaluate your goals before you begin negotiations with prospective buyers. You have several advantages when you understand the consequences of each decision and make choices based on that understanding.

Types of goals to have clear in your mind include:

- Knowledge of the minimum price you will accept.
- Awareness of the type of terms to which you will agree.
- Items to be on the alert for in negotiating.

Consider Price and Terms

Consider both the price and your acceptable terms when you negotiate. The following chart indicates that *if*:

- Seller and buyers are both primarily interested in price, they rarely sign a contract.
- A seller is primarily concerned with terms and buyers are mainly concerned with price, they generally sign a contract.
- A seller is primarily concerned with price and buyers are mainly concerned with terms, they usually sign a contract.

• Seller and buyers both have the greatest concern about terms, they generally reach an agreement, too.

		Seller	
		PRICE	TERMS
Buyer	Price	No agreement	Agreement
	Terms	Agreement	Agreement

Prepare Negotiating Goals Worksheet

The Goals/Negotiating Goals Worksheet in Section VI, "Worksheets and Contracts" helps make your priorities in negotiating the sale of your home clear to you.

1. Write out all of the goals you wish to achieve relating to negotiating the sale of your home.
2. Prioritize the goals you listed by placing a number to the left of each goal. (Make the most important goal 1, the second most important goal 2, and so on.)
3. Rewrite your goals in their order of importance. This prioritized goals list provides you with a reference as you negotiate the sale of your home.

Prepare Estimate of Proceeds Worksheet—Preliminary

To get a clear idea of how much you plan to receive from selling your home, prepare the Estimate of Proceeds Worksheet—Preliminary in Section VI, "Worksheets and Contracts."

1. Enter the information requested at the top of each page.
2. Check the costs you intend to pay when you sell your home.
   • *Appraisal fee:* Cost for hiring an appraiser to determine the current market value of your property in order to make a loan to the buyers. Buyers usually pay.
   • *Assessments:* Taxes or charges by a governmental body in addition to normal property taxes for a property owner's proportionate cost of specific improvements, such as schools, streets, and sewers. You and buyers usually pay your prorated share of assessments.
   • *Assumption fee (transfer fee):* A charge for the work involved to transfer the mortgage from you to buyers. Buyers generally pay.

- *Attorney's fees (legal fees):* Charges by an attorney for legal advice and/or assistance. Whoever hires the attorney usually pays. If you hire an attorney to assist you with your home sale, you pay unless you negotiate otherwise. If the matter is decided by a court of law, then the person against whose favor the case is decided must pay the fees.

- *Beneficiary statement:* A statement provided by a lender using a trust deed type of loan. On this statement a lender usually lists the remaining principal balance, interest payments, loan due dates, terms of payment, insurance data, taxes, assessments, and any other claims that do not appear on trust deed documents. Whoever handles the closing usually requires a beneficiary statement when buyers take over a trust deed. You generally pay.

- *Credit report:* Charge for a detailed report of buyers' credit history. Lenders usually require a credit report before making a loan to buyers. Lenders may include this charge as part of a loan fee. Buyers usually pay.

- *Delinquent payments:* Failure to make loan payments when they are due. You usually pay.

- *Demand fee (demand for payoff charge):* A fee for a written request to a lender for the lender's demand for the payment of the loan in full and the supporting documents necessary for release of the lien against the property. Demands are used if you intend to pay off the existing loan in full. You usually pay.

- *Document preparation:* Charges for drawing up and preparing legal papers. The party that pays generally depends on the type of document being prepared. You typically pay for preparation of documents in favor of (to) the buyers.

- *Drawing deed:* A fee for the preparation of a deed. The party that pays depends on the type of deed prepared. The party that benefits from the deed generally pays.

- *Escrow/closing fees:* Charges paid to the escrow holder or closing agent for handling the escrow or closing. Usually split evenly between you and the buyers.

- *Homeowner's association fees:* Monthly fees owners of homes pay to their homeowner's association. These dues can be for such items as maintenance, gardening, trash collection, outside lighting, pool, spa, and tennis courts. These dues are generally prorated.

- *Homeowner's insurance:* Insurance protection against stated specific hazards, such as fire, hail, windstorms, earthquakes, floods, civil disturbances, explosions, riots, theft, and vandalism. Lenders usually require at least minimum coverage to protect their interest in a property. The lender's interest in the property is the balance of the loan that has not yet been paid. Buyers usually pay.

- *Home warranty:* Fee for insurance that the items listed in the contract (such as plumbing, wiring, water heater, and major appliances) are in working order for the specified length of time. Traditionally, you pay.
- *Impounds (reserve fund):* Funds held by the lender to assure payment in the future of recurring expenses. This money is generally held in a trust-type account. These expenses can include FHA mortgage premiums, insurance premiums, real estate taxes, and sewer and water taxes. Impounds are generally prorated. If you have prepaid these expenses, you should receive the excess at the close of escrow. If, however, you have not paid these expenses, you will be charged for your portion of the costs.
- *Interest:* A charge or rate paid to a lender for borrowing money. Interest on existing loans is paid from the last monthly payment until the closing date. Interest is paid after the charge is incurred (in arrears). Interest on an existing loan is usually prorated.
- *Loan origination fee:* Lender's charge for arranging and processing a loan. The fee is usually based on a percentage of the loan. Buyers typically pay.
- *Loan tie-in fee:* A fee charged by whoever handles the closing or escrow for their work and liability in conforming to the lender's criteria for the buyers' new loan. Buyers generally pay.
- *Notary fee:* A charge paid to a notary public to guarantee signatures on some of the legal documents in the transaction.
- *Pest control inspection (structural pest control inspection fee, termite inspection fee):* The cost of the inspection of your property by a licensed pest control inspector for infestation or infections by wood-destroying organisms. You generally pay.
- *Pest control repair charge (structural pest control repair charge):* Cost of repairing any damage done by infestation or infection of property by wood-destroying organisms. You usually pay all charges, unless you negotiate or use a contract that states otherwise.
- *Physical inspection fee (home inspection fee):* A fee for a study of the property's site, structures, systems, and appliances. Buyers usually pay.
- *Points (discount points, loan discount fee):* A one-time charge by the lender to adjust the yield on the loan to current market

conditions or to adjust the rate on the loan to the level required by federal or state regulations. Each point is equal to 1 percent of the loan balance. This fee is treated as prepaid interest for tax purposes. Buyers usually pay; however, you are legally required to pay VA discount points.

- *Prepayment penalty:* The fine imposed on a borrower by a lender for the early payoff of a loan or any substantial part of a loan. You usually pay.
- *Property taxes (taxes):* The amount of the tax usually depends on the amount of the valuation of the property. You typically pay for property taxes due but not yet paid.
- *Reconveyance fee:* A fee charged for the deed filed at the county recorder's office to record payment in full of a trust deed and transfer legal title from the trustee to you. You usually pay.
- *Recording fee:* Fee charged for the entry of your transaction into the official records at the county recorder's office. You usually pay for the recording of documents in favor of buyers. Buyers generally pay for the recording of documents in favor of the lender.
- *Satisfaction of mortgage:* A document signed by the holder of the mortgage that indicates you have paid your mortgage off in full. You generally pay.
- *Subescrow fee:* A fee charged by a title company for the firm's costs and liability when it handles money. You usually pay.
- *Survey fee:* Charge for a survey showing the exact location and boundaries of a property. Buyers usually pay.
- *Title insurance:* A policy for protection against claims in the future based on circumstances in the past. This type of insurance is issued by the title company on completion of the final title search. Title insurance coverage requirements vary depending on the need of the parties (seller, buyers, and lender) for a specific type of coverage, the amount of money each of the parties will pay for coverage, the type of property covered, complexity of the transaction, and exceptions and encumbrances to the title.
  - *Basic coverage:* All title insurance has basic coverage, including matters of public record such as encumbrances, liens, and judgments; forgery and fraud; lack of capacity (persons not being able to enter into a contract because they are minors or not of sound mind); and improper delivery (the deed has not met the criteria for proper delivery).
  - *Standard coverage insurance:* The regular investigation for standard insurance reveals only matters of record and the location of the improvements with respect to the lot line.

These matters include access to public streets; defects in the title; charges, claims, or liens on the title; inability to sell the property because of unacceptable encumbrances on the title; and vesting (interest that cannot be revoked) being other than stated. You or buyers may pay for standard coverage depending on what you negotiated or local customs. Standard owner's (joint protection) policy provides insurance to the buyers and the lender. Standard lender's policy provides coverage for the lender only.

- ○ *Extended coverage insurance:* Extended coverage protects against numerous risks that are not a matter of record. This coverage usually requires a survey, which includes a thorough search, checking with government agencies, and on-site field work. Extended coverage policies generally cost considerably more than standard policies. These policies insure against all risks insured against by the standard policy *plus* claims not previously disclosed by examination of public record. Buyers usually pay for an extended coverage owner's policy.
- ○ *Special endorsements:* Special endorsements are clauses used to modify, expand, or delete the coverage of any policy.
- *Title search fee (title examination fee):* A charge for the examination of information recorded on your property at the county recorder's office. This examination is to verify that the property has no outstanding claims or liens against it that could adversely affect the buyers or lender. It also verifies that you can transfer clear legal title to the property. The party that pays traditionally depends on the customs in your area.
- *Transfer tax (documentary transfer tax):* A tax that some states allow individual counties or cities to charge on the transfer of real property, including homes. This tax is often based on the amount of equity being transferred to the buyers. You typically pay.
- *Other fees:* Include fees you use that are not on the previous list.

3. Obtain estimates for items you checked from sources listed.
   a. Costs
      - Appraisal fee—Local appraisers or lenders.
      - Assessments—Your property tax bill.
      - Assumption fee—The lender who made your home loan.
      - Attorney's fees—Local attorneys or the local bar association.
      - Beneficiary statement fee—The lender who made your home loan.

- Credit report—Lender who made your home loan or other local lenders.
- Delinquent payments—Lender who made your home loan.
- Demand fees—Lender who made your home loan.
- Document preparation fees—Whomever you want to handle closing, such as your lawyer, escrow or title company, or the escrow department of your bank.
- Drawing deed—Whomever you want to do the closing, such as your lawyer, the escrow department of your bank, or an escrow or title company.
- Escrow/closing fees—Whomever you want to do the closing, such as your lawyer, the escrow department of your bank, or an escrow company.
- Homeowner's association fees—Your homeowner's association.
- Homeowner's insurance—The company that currently insures your house.
- Home warranty—Home warranty companies, represented locally.
- Impounds—Lender who made your home loan.
- Interest—Lender who made your home loan.
- Loan origination fee—Local lenders.
- Loan tie-in fee—Local escrow companies or the person whom you plan to have handle closing.
- Notary fee—The person or company you plan to have handle closing or escrow.
- Pest control inspection—Local pest control companies.
- Pest control repair charge—Local pest control companies.
- Physical inspection fee—Local home inspection companies.
- Points—Local lenders.
- Prepayment penalty—Lender who made your loan.
- Property taxes—Your property tax bill.
- Reconveyance fee—Trustee on your trust deed.
- Recording fee—Your county recorder or the person whom you want to handle the closing.
- Satisfaction of mortgage—Lender on your mortgage.
- Subescrow fee—Local title companies.
- Survey fee—Local survey companies.
- Title insurance—Local title insurance companies.
- Title search fee—Local title insurance companies.
- Transfer tax—Whomever you want to handle closing, such as your lawyer, the escrow department of your bank, or an escrow or title company.

4. Decide the expenses that you feel will be prorated. Prorations are adjustments to the amount owed by you and the buyers.

These adjustments must be made because escrow rarely transfers title exactly corresponding to the paid-up dates of expenses, such as assessments, bonds, homeowner's association dues, impound accounts, insurance premiums, interest on existing loans, maintenance fees, property taxes, and rental payments. Buyers owe you for any time period after escrow closes for which you have already paid. You owe buyers for any time period before escrow closes for which you have not yet paid. For this estimate, base prorations on a 360-day year of 12 months, each containing 30 days.

5. Check the monetary encumbrances (claims or charges against a property) that exist against your property.
   - First, second, or third loans (mortgages or trust deeds).
   - Improvement bond (a debt secured by a government loan financing improvements within a district).
   - Liens (charges against property for the payment of a debt or obligation).
   - Other (such items as delinquent property taxes).

6. Check which of the estimated credits you feel will be due to you. These items will be the prorations for which buyers owe you because you have already paid.

7. Add each column separately to obtain total estimated amounts for each column.

8. Add total estimated costs and total estimated encumbrances to obtain estimated debits.

9. Calculate your net proceeds from your proposed home sale.
   a. Enter your proposed selling price.
   b. Subtract total estimated debits.
   c. Enter the subtotal.
   d. Add the total estimated credits.
   e. Obtain your estimate of proceeds from the proposed sale.

10. If you plan to finance a note for buyers and you want to estimate how much cash you might receive in that case:
    a. Enter the amount you plan to finance.
    b. Subtract the amount you plan to finance from your estimate of proceeds.
    c. Enter the difference, which is the estimate of cash from such a sale.

Step 2: Set up Offer Presentation

When?

Choose a time for an offer presentation when you are at your best, a time when:

- You are rested, calm, and feeling well.
- You are able to have an offer presentation conference in a convenient and unhurried manner.
- You have reviewed not only what price and terms you will consider but also how to conduct the negotiation.

Where?

Have buyers present their offer at your clutter-free dining room or kitchen table. Maintain a quiet, businesslike atmosphere in this area during the discussion.

How?

Consider:

1. Informing everyone concerned about the exact location and time of the offer presentation.
2. After everyone arrives, introducing everyone who is present and explaining each of their roles in the offer presentation.
3. Insisting on seeing a written offer signed by buyers before you negotiate.
4. Giving buyers a copy of the disclosure statement and all inspection reports issued in the last two years on your home before they make the offer.

For multiple offers in a short time period, you might have buyers make offer presentations in the order that the buyers contacted you. Legally you can consider offers in any order in most areas. Maintaining the order may discourage hard feelings or unfounded charges by some potential buyers.

Step 3: Handle the Offer Presentation

Handle the offer presentation so that it works well for you.

Manage Offer Presentation

To manage the offer presentation to your best advantage:

1. Have buyers or their agent make the offer presentation.
2. Be aware of some possible buyers' techniques. Some buyers may use a number of subtle but often powerful techniques to attempt to make you feel ill at ease and negotiate less effectively. If you recognize these techniques, you may be able to avoid their pressure.
   - Buyers arrive late for your meeting.
     a. Remain calm if buyers are late. Becoming upset may cost you money.

    b. If buyers are more than 20 minutes late or you become upset, consider rescheduling the meeting for another mutually agreeable time.

- Buyers make a telephone call when you are meeting.
  a. Request that they make the call after the meeting.
  b. Ask to set up the appointment for a time that would be more convenient for you both.
- Buyers seem to care less about buying your home than you do about selling it; they appear disinterested.
  a. Remain objective.
  b. Be prepared to make a counteroffer.
  c. Sign only agreements with which you are comfortable.
  d. Talk only to your consultants about the agreement you are negotiating. You will not be embarrassed if the agreement changes or does not go through.
  e. Spend money only after you receive it so you do not force yourself to accept costly changes.
- Buyers make misleading or incorrect statements.
  a. Only believe what you hear if it is verified by someone without an interest in the transaction.
  b. Obtain a written copy of the statement signed by the buyers.
- Buyers voice their opinions about things they feel are wrong with your property.
  a. Realize that buyers are trying to unnerve you and better their own bargaining position.
  b. Remain calm.
- Buyers make many notes.
  a. Understand that buyers may think that making many notes will unnerve you.
  b. Remain calm.
- Buyers may get too close to you for your comfort.
  a. Recognize that buyers may be trying to take your mind off the negotiations.
  b. If you are bothered, ask them to move away.
- Buyers may use statements that seem to sound authoritative.
  a. Understand buyers are seldom authorities; they may be opinionated or trying to cover up their own ignorance.
  b. Ask questions, even if you fear buyers may think that you don't know the answers.
  c. Remember, the price or terms you get for your property may depend on your response.

- Buyers may try to pressure you into making an agreement at the last minute by appealing to your emotions using dramatic actions and words.
   a. Recognize that buyers may be attempting to play on your emotions.
   b. Tell buyers you need time to consider the offer.
3. Study each section of the offer carefully, particularly:
   - The contingencies listed in the offer.
   - The time limits set by the buyers. Time limits should be adequate but not needlessly long.
4. Ask questions about each point covered in the contract that you are unsure of or do not understand.
5. Allow buyers or their agent to answer your questions and fully explain each point.
6. Inform buyers or their agent that you want time to consider the offer.
   a. Thank buyers courteously for their offer.
   b. Tell buyers you will consider their offer.
   c. Inform buyers you will let them know your decision within three business days (or an appropriate time limit under the circumstances). Consider never rejecting buyers' offers immediately.
   d. Take your time and prepare a counteroffer.
   e. Remember that negotiation is a give-and-take process.
7. If you decide to negotiate, remember these tips:
   - Use logic to explain the soundness of your requests.
   - Compromise: exchange a buyers' request for one of your own.
8. If you decide to accept the buyers' offer:
   - Accept a written offer *only,* to prevent any questions from arising later as to when the contract was signed.
   - Sign your acceptance on the same form on which the offer was made.

Be Aware of Revocation Possibility

Be aware that an offer may be revoked (called back) in writing by buyers at any time before you communicate to buyers that you have accepted their offer.

After you have prepared for the negotiation, you are ready to study the contract in detail so that you understand it well.

10

Understand Purchase Contracts

An important aspect of achieving your goals is your familiarity with the form you will be using. Your understanding of this form and ability to fill it in to accurately reflect your decisions are essential in saving you money and anxiety in the sale of your home.

Step 1: Learn about Contracts

Note that the following priorities exist in contracts in most states in the event of discrepancies or inconsistencies:

- Written words usually take precedence over printed and typed wording.
- Typed words generally take precedence over printed wording but not over written wording.
- Specific provisions in a contract usually supersede the general provisions.
- A real estate purchase contract normally takes precedence over escrow instructions, if the two do not agree.

Step 2: Understand Purchase Contract

A purchase contract is the basic agreement between you and buyers for their purchase of your home. Many variations of this form exist. We present a generic Purchase Contract in Section VI, "Worksheets and Contracts."

1. Study the form presented, which gives you a comprehensive generic sampling of purchase contracts' contents.
2. Check with your consultants to obtain a copy of the type of purchase contract used in your area.
3. Ask your consultants if you have questions regarding:
   - Differences between the forms.
   - Applicability of sections you feel you might want to include in your contract.

We explain, as appropriate, the form's expected responses, possible choices, and probable consequences, as well as give our recommendations.

When you fill out a form, consider filling in each blank with either the specific information you desire to convey or with the words *not applicable* as appropriate, so that no information can be added later. The only spaces that should be left blank are those requiring signatures and dates. If you amend a contract later, make the changes on a separate sheet.

Completing the Contract Preliminaries

Sum

The "sum of" wording asks for the monetary amount as a number.

Dollars

Dollars followed by the blank for the dollar amount requests an amount written as numbers.

Evidence of Payment

- Cash—Count cash several times and give a receipt to the buyer. Obtain a receipt for the exact amount when you deposit it with the closing agent or escrow holder.
- Cashier's check—A bank's own check guaranteed to be good by that bank.
- Personal check—Buyers usually use a personal check for the initial deposit. Be aware that buyers may not have sufficient funds in their personal account when you try to cash their check.
- Jewelry, furniture, works of art, and so on—You may accept these items as partial or full deposit. We do not recommend them because they are difficult to identify, set a value on, and in some cases store.

Payable To

Consider asking buyers to make out a check to the closing agent or escrow holder (often a title or escrow company) on which you and buyers agree. This action should prevent any accusation by buyers that you have misused funds.

Completing Item 1: Fixtures

Fixtures and fittings are considered items that are permanently attached to or for which special openings have been made in your home and its associated structures. They are included in the purchase price and are transferred with the home unless you and the buyers agree specifically to exclude certain items.

Completing Item 2: Personal Property

Personal property is considered items that are not permanently attached to your home or other structures on your property. Items of personal property that you list here you include in the sale of your home. These listed items are free of any liens against them (money owed or rights of others regarding the items). You do not guarantee the condition of the items you list.

Completing Item 3: Property Condition

You guarantee through the date you make possession available to the buyers that:

- You will maintain property and improvements in the same condition as on the date you accepted the buyers' offer.
- The roof is free of all known leaks, and all systems and built-in appliances operate.
- You will replace all broken and cracked glass.

Completing Item 4: Seller Representation

You guarantee that you have no knowledge of any notice of violations of any codes or ordinances or other regulations filed or issued against the property by any department of any governmental body. You will give notice if you gain such knowledge until date escrow closes.

Completing Item 5: Supplements

Supplements are contracts that are incorporated in an agreement, although they are not written on the same form as the agreement. Supplements include those described here.

Interim Occupancy Agreement

The interim occupancy agreement is a lease purchase agreement used to rent your home *to* the buyers *before* the sale. For more information on lease purchase agreements, see Chapter 12, "Understand Other Possible Offers."

Residential Lease Agreement after Sale

A residential lease agreement after sale is a sale leaseback agreement used to lease your former home *from* the buyers *after* the sale. For more information on sale leaseback agreements, see Chapter 12, "Understand Other Possible Offers."

VA and FHA Amendments

These amendments are on a form used to describe financial arrangements when buyers are getting a new VA or FHA loan on the property.

Residential Lease Option

Consider using lease options and purchase option agreements under the appropriate circumstances. The lease option, or lease with an option to buy, is a combination lease, purchase contract, and option. Use a lease option form if you and potential buyers make an agreement that includes:

- You leasing your property to buyers for the specified rental payment.
- Buyers having the right and the option to purchase your home for the amount listed in the contract within the period of time agreed on by you and buyers.
- Buyers paying you a lease option fee if they do not purchase the property. See Chapter 12, "Understand Other Possible Offers," for further information.

Real Estate Purchase Option

A purchase option or option to buy is a combination purchase contract and option. Use a purchase option if you and buyers negotiate a contract in which buyers agree to:

- Make the purchase within the listed period of time, *if* they decide to buy the property.
- Purchase the property for the amount listed and under the terms in the contract, *if* they decide to buy your home.
- Pay an option fee to you if they do not use the option. See Chapter 12, "Understand Other Possible Offers," for further information.

Completing Item 6: Escrow

Escrow is a process by which you and buyers deposit documents and/or money with a neutral third party. You both give instructions for the third party to hold and disburse documents and funds after certain listed conditions are met.

Delivery of Escrow Instructions

Lenders in many areas often require an escrow as a condition for making a loan. Institutional lenders, such as banks and savings and loans, have escrow departments within their own organizations. Other escrow holders include attorneys and real estate brokers. The choice of an escrow holder is negotiable between you and the buyers. Consider choosing an escrow holder who handles many of these transactions each year. That party is most likely to be competent.

Time Limit

The amount of time until closing depends on the steps necessary:

- Within 45 to 60 days from your acceptance is usually considered sufficient time.
- For houses on which new FHA or VA loans must be obtained, allow about 90 days after your acceptance of the buyers' offer to close of escrow.
- For transactions that are all cash or in which the necessary inspections were performed before signing the contract, 20 days after your acceptance of the buyers' offer may be all that is required.

Escrow Fees

Escrow fees are negotiable. You and buyers usually split this cost equally.

Completing Item 7: Occupancy

Occupancy information is for lenders. Lenders offer a better rate on a property occupied by the owner.

Completing Item 8: Possession

Possession means that buyers may physically move into the property.

Close of Escrow

Indicate whether you and buyers agree that buyers get possession at close of escrow. At close of escrow is the time title usually transfers to the buyers. You can:

- Move out of your home *before* close of escrow. The house is available for buyers to move into immediately after close of escrow, so that you do not owe buyers any money. You must make all payments on the home you are selling up to the close of escrow, as well as paying for wherever you are staying in the meantime.
- Move out of your home *at* the close of escrow. In this way you are not paying for two places to stay. The exact date for the

close of escrow is often difficult to determine. Even if a date is set, it may change.

Not Later Than

At the close of escrow title usually transfers to buyers. You pay buyers rent from the day escrow closes until you actually move out. Rent is usually computed on a daily basis. The advantage is you are not paying for two places to stay. The disadvantage is the rent you pay is based on buyers' cost of ownership, which is usually more than your cost when it was your own home.

Three days after the close of escrow is usually sufficient time to allow you to move out.

Other Possession Arrangements

Avoid renting your home to buyers or even allowing them to move a few things into the house before escrow closes:

- Buyers have less incentive to complete escrow if they are living in your home. They may live in your home at less cost than they will pay after the purchase.
- Buyers may find many small things not to their liking and try to avoid purchasing your home.
- Buyers may be difficult to remove from your home if escrow should fail.

Completing Item 9: Keys

You must provide buyers keys and/or means to operate (such as combinations) all locks and alarms on the property on the possession date.

Completing Item 10: Financing

This contract depends on buyers obtaining financing.

A. Diligence and Good Faith

You must rely on buyers to act with diligence and good faith to obtain financing. Consider requiring buyers to prequalify for loans before you sign an agreement with them.

Time Limits. Thirty days after the opening of escrow is generally sufficient time for buyers to obtain all applicable financing.

B. Deposit

Wherever you live, consider requiring a deposit (earnest money) from buyers as evidence of their intention and ability to buy in exchange for tying up your property by signing a contract with buyers. In theory, if buyers default, they forfeit the deposit. Failing to make a good-faith effort to remove contingencies or backing out of a contract without good reason are generally considered defaults.

In practice, because home purchase contracts usually contain contingency clauses, buyers seldom forfeit deposits to sellers. Sellers also seldom receive forfeited deposits because title and escrow companies rarely release deposit money without the written consent of both parties.

Still, we recommend deposits. Most buyers are much more likely to act in good faith to attempt to buy your property if they made a substantial deposit.

Deposited Into. Consider choosing an escrow holder who handles many of these transactions each year to hold the deposit. This escrow holder is most likely to give you the best service and price. Institutional lenders, such as banks and savings and loans, often have escrow departments within their own organizations. Other escrow holders include attorneys and real estate brokers.

Amount of Deposit. The amount of the initial deposit is often $500 to $5,000 or more, depending on the price of your home and the amount common in your area.

C. Increased Deposit

Depending on the amount of the initial deposit, buyers may increase the deposit by a specified date. Buyers usually increase a deposit to demonstrate that they are serious about wanting to purchase your home.

Time Limit. Usually, on or before 10 to 14 days after your acceptance is ample time for the buyers to increase the deposit.

Deposited Into. Generally you designate *escrow* or *the closing agent* as the receiver of the funds.

Amount of Increased Deposit. The amount of the increased deposit, if any, depends on what you negotiate with the buyers. For example, the buyers may have some questions about your home. They will offer you a small initial deposit and agree to pay you the balance of a larger amount of deposit after certain conditions are met. These conditions might include a clear preliminary title report or a clear termite report.

D. Down Payment Balance

Down payment is the money you and the buyers agree on or that a lender requires buyers to pay toward the purchase price before escrow can close. A deposit is generally part, but not all, of the down payment. Buyers usually pay the final amount of the down payment on or before a particular date *or* before the occurrence of a specified action, such as the close of escrow.

If you will be carrying a loan from the buyers or are remaining primarily or secondarily liable for the loan, consider weighing the advantages and disadvantages of different amounts of down payment. Decide on a range of down payments within which you are comfortable selling your home. See Chapter 3, "Determine Your Financial Requirements," for more information regarding down payments.

Deposited Into. Usually you designate *escrow* or *with the closing agent.*

Time Limit. Specified date or the occurrence of a certain action, such as the closing of escrow.

Amount of Down Payment Balance. The final amount of the down payment. This amount is often the sum needed to make the total deposit equal to 5 to 25 percent of the purchase price, for example.

Price of house	$ 150,000
Percentage down payment	× 0.10
Total down payment needed	$ 15,000
Total down payment needed	$ 15,000
Less deposit	− 1,000
Less increased deposit	− 2,000
Balance of down payment	$ 12,000

E. New First Loan

Buyers will apply for, qualify for, and obtain a new first loan (mortgage or trust deed). Buyers may need to secure a new first loan for one of the following reasons:

- You currently have no first loan on your home.
- You or the lender are not willing for the buyer to assume or take title subject to an existing loan.

Loan Type. The buyers choose the type of loan they want to obtain to purchase your home.

- Fixed rate loan—A loan on which the percentage of interest remains at the same rate and payments of principal remain equal over the life of the loan.
- Adjustable rate loan—A loan that allows periodic adjustments in interest rate. This loan adjusts at a specified time based on a named index.

Loan Fee Maximum. Loan fees are one-time charges by lenders for initiating a loan. Buyers are usually willing to pay no more than 3 percent of the loan amount in loan fees. Loan fees usually include points, appraisal costs, and charges for credit checks.

Discount Points. Each discount point is equal to 1 percent of the loan total. This fee is paid to the lender when the lender makes the loan. Federal regulations require the seller to pay VA discount points. Buyer or seller may pay FHA discount points, depending on what you negotiate.

Additional Terms. Consider including:

- The stipulation that buyers must qualify for a loan within 10 days from the opening of escrow.
- The designation of who pays which loan fees. These fees generally include the costs for points (loan origination fees), an appraisal, and a credit check. See the discussion of these costs later in the chapter.
- If your house does not appraise at the value on which you and buyers agreed, you have several options:
  - Buyers may pay for the difference between the appraisal and the purchase price.
  - You both may renegotiate the price of the home.
  - You both may revoke (cancel) the contract.

F. Existing First Loan

If you will allow buyers to assume or take title subject to an existing first (most senior) loan, use this section.

Assuming and Taking Title Subject To. Be sure you understand the effects of allowing buyers to assume or take title subject to an existing first loan.

- Assume—Buyers take over primary responsibility for the payment of the existing loan and primary liability for any deficiency judgment arising from it. You become secondarily liable for the loan and for any deficiency judgment arising from it. A deficiency judgment makes an individual personally liable for the payoff of a remaining amount due because less than the full amount was obtained by foreclosure.
- Take title subject to—Buyers take over responsibility for payment on an existing loan without taking on the liability of a deficiency judgment. You remain primarily responsible for the loan and any deficiency judgment arising from it.

Approximate Balance. Give an estimate of the amount you owe on the first loan.

Interest Rate. The *current* rate of interest on the loan. For information about fixed rate and adjustable rate loans, see item 10E under Loan Type earlier in this chapter.

Loan Fee Maximum. Give the maximum loan fee. For information regarding loan fees, see item 10E under Loan Fee Maximum earlier in this chapter. For disposition of the impound account, indicate how you want the account handled. *Impound accounts* are trust accounts established by lenders to accumulate funds to meet certain debts. These debts may include taxes, premiums on homeowner's insurance policies, and FHA mortgage insurance premiums. Lenders usually collect these funds along with note payments, then place funds in a trust account. The contents of impound accounts are generally prorated as of the close of escrow. You and buyers may negotiate another date if you wish.

Additional Terms. Indicate additional terms you want included.

G. Note Secured by Trust Deed

You can act as a lender to carry back (hold) loans from buyers. These notes may be first, second, or even third loans. They may be mortgages or trust deeds, depending on the type of loan used in your area. For details regarding seller carry-back loans, see Chapter 3, "Determine Your Financial Requirements."

Deeds of Trust. If buyers plan to obtain money for the purchase as more than one loan, use this section for the most senior loan. Indicate the seniority of the loan (first, second, or third). Place information regarding any other notes secured by mortgages or trust deeds that you may make to buyers in an additional financing terms section of the agreement.

Interest Rate. For the interest rate on a loan in favor of the seller, consider checking with your escrow holder or title representative regarding federally required and assigned (imputed) interest rules before entering a percentage in this blank. Federally imputed interest rate rules are for federal income tax calculations only. If you do not charge a federally set minimum interest rate on a loan, the federal government taxes you as if you had charged the minimum. Consult your tax preparer or accountant for further details.

Due Date. Consider using a due date or similar due-on-sale clause in a loan. It not only makes the loan due at a specific time but also gives you the right to call (demand payment of) all sums owed immediately due and payable if buyers sell or otherwise transfer title. You may then decide whether to continue the loan with the new owners or request the loan be paid off.

Late Charge. A late charge is often set at 5 to 10 percent of the usual payment by sellers. The charge is negotiable. The number of days following the due date after which a late charge will be added is negotiable. Sellers often request 5 to 15 days.

Request for Notice of Default or Sale. Making sure the loan (trust deed or mortgage) contains a notice of default or sale is for your benefit.

- If buyers default on loan, you will know to make the payments on the senior loan to protect your investment.
- If buyers sell the property, you will be notified so you can collect the money owed to you on the loan.

Request for Notice of Delinquency. Buyers have the choice of whether to execute (sign) a request for notice of delinquency, although they may ask for your advice. Advising buyers when their payment is late is more work for you, but informing them can be worth the effort if it helps remind buyers to make payments they forgot.

Additional Terms. If you checked *or upon sale or transfer of the subject property,* consider using a prepayment penalty, the fine imposed on buyers for repaying a loan early.

H. New Second Loan

Buyers may want or need a new second loan for several reasons:

- Buyers do not have sufficient ready cash to pay up to the amount of the first loan.
- You or the lender would not be willing for buyers to assume or take title subject to the existing second loan.
- Buyers may be able to obtain a loan at a lower interest rate than the rate of the loan you currently have.

Type of Loan. See item 10E under Type of Loan earlier in this chapter.

Loan Fee. See item 10E under Loan Fee Maximum earlier in this chapter.

Additional Terms. See item 10E under Additional Terms earlier in this chapter.

I. Existing Second Loan

If you are willing to have buyers assume or take title subject to an existing second loan, use this section. You can eliminate this contingency by:

1. Obtaining lender's permission for buyers to assume your second loan or take title subject to your first loan.
2. Requiring buyers to prequalify with the lender to assume or take title subject to your second loan.

Information regarding the buyer assuming or taking title to an existing loan is the same as for an existing first loan, described earlier in item F.

Interest Rate. Enter the *current* rate of interest on the loan, no matter what type of loan is involved.

Type of Loan. See item 10E under Type of Loan earlier in this chapter.

J. Other Provisions

If buyers assume or take title subject to an existing loan, you must provide buyers with copies of documents that apply to that loan for the buyer to approve or disapprove.

Time Limit. Ten calendar days after buyers receive copies of documents that apply to the loan is considered ample time for buyers to notify you in writing of their disapproval.

Loan Balance Difference Adjustment. You and the buyers may agree on one or several methods to adjust (make up the difference) between the estimated and actual amounts of the existing loan. These methods include the buyer paying cash for the difference, the lender changing the loan amount to include the difference, or you carrying back financing for the difference. See Chapter 3, "Determine Your Financial Requirements" regarding seller carry-back financing.

K. Additional Financing Terms

Enter any other financing terms that are too lengthy to fit into another section or do not apply to other sections. These terms might include several items:

- *All Inclusive Trust Deed (AITD, Wraparound Mortgage, Overriding Deed of Trust):* A junior loan at one overall interest rate used to wrap existing mortgages or trust deeds into a package. The amount is sufficient to cover the existing loan and provide extra for you, the seller. You make payments on existing loan(s) from buyers' payments. You remain primarily responsible for the mortgages or trust deeds wrapped. See Chapter 3, "Determine Your Financial Requirements," for more details regarding these loans.
- *Seller Buy-Down:* A loan in which the effective interest rate is bought down or reduced during the beginning years of the loan by your contributions. You are really paying buyers' interest in advance. This lower interest rate usually lasts two or three years. You may increase the price to cover this added cost. See Chapter 3, "Determine Your Financial Requirements," for more information.

Completing Item 11: Title

Title insurance protects parties to the sale against claims in the future based on circumstances in the past.

Title insurance coverages vary depending on the needs of the parties (you, buyers, and lender) for a particular coverage, amount of money each is willing to pay, type of property covered, complexity of the transaction, and exceptions and encumbrances to the title. See Chapter 9, "Prepare for Negotiation," for further information regarding title insurance.

Time Limit

Within 10 calendar days of receipt of the current preliminary title report is usually ample time for buyers to disapprove the report in writing.

Expense

The party that traditionally pays title insurance fees depends on the customs in your area. Check with your local lender, title representative, or escrow officer if you are unsure.

Completing Item 12: Vesting

Vesting, the manner in which buyers hold title, may have significant legal and tax consequences. Each method of holding title has certain advantages and disadvantages, depending on the buyers' situation and objectives.

Vesting of Title

If buyers ask you how they should vest title, suggest they consult their attorney.

Completing Item 13: Prorations

Prorations distribute responsibility for payment of expenses of home ownership. This distribution is based on the percentage of an assessment or billing period during which you and buyers own the property. Prorations may be calculated as of any mutually agreeable date.

Items usually prorated include property taxes, insurance premiums, interest on loans, homeowner dues, and rents. Other items may be prorated if you and buyers agree.

Proration Date

Date options for prorations include but are not limited to the date the deed is recorded in the country recorder's office, the date of the close of escrow, or the date of possession (the date buyers may physically move into the property).

Bonds and Assessments

The party that pays bonds or assessments is negotiable. Generally you pay bonds or assessments that are now a lien, whereas payments that are not yet due are assumed by buyers.

Although you may pay most bonds and assessments in full, including all payments not yet due, some liens must be assumed because they legally cannot be paid off. Liens that must be assumed are often treated as a credit to buyers in escrow or a reduction of the purchase price.

County Transfer Tax

Transfer tax or documentary transfer fee is a tax that some states allow individual counties and/or cities to place on the transferral of real property, including homes. Tax stamps, used in some areas, are a method of showing that a transfer tax has been paid. Buyers generally pay for tax stamps. These stamps are then attached to the deed to prove that the tax has been paid.

Whether buyers or sellers pay the tax is negotiable. You traditionally pay, although some states may have laws requiring buyers to pay in certain types of sales. Check with your escrow holder or attorney regarding the laws in your state.

Other Transfer Tax

In some states, counties and cities may each impose their own documentary transfer tax. Whether buyers or sellers pay the tax is negotiable. You typically pay this tax. Check with a closing agent, escrow holder, or attorney to see:

- *If* there is a transfer tax or stamp tax required.
- The rate of taxation for each transfer tax required.
- What amount is considered to be taxable.

Completing Item 14: Tax Withholding

A federal law ensuring that foreign nationals who sell property in the United States pay capital gains tax on their profit makes buyers responsible for the collection of those taxes.

Buyers may ask you to sign an affidavit stating that you are *not* a nonresident alien for the purposes of U.S. income taxation in order to comply with FIRPTA regulations. FIRPTA is the Foreign Investment in Real Property Tax Act. This act requires *buyers* to deduct and withhold 10 percent of the sales price to pay the tax *unless* an exemption applies.

See Chapter 17, "Handle Taxes," for more details.

Completing Item 15: Other Terms and Conditions

Enter items in this section that:

- Might not logically be included in any other section.
- Place conditions on a section that is already included but in which there is not sufficient space to insert those conditions. Be sure to:
    1. List the section number, letter, and name designation before listing the conditions.
    2. Indicate under the appropriate section to *See Section 15*.

Conditions you might consider including (and that are described elsewhere in this book) are beneficiary statements (demands), drawing of documents, judgments, and notary fees.

Completing Item 17: Entire Contract

Time is important. That is, some actions required by this contract cannot be taken until other actions required by the contract are performed.

Completing Item 18: Amendments

After you have signed a contract, do not write on the form. The contract should not be changed except by *another agreement* in written form and signed by both you and the buyers.

Completing Item 19: Offer

The offer is to buy the property described. The offer is considered revoked unless the listed conditions are met.

Time Limit

Five calendar days is usually considered sufficient time from the date of the offer that unless the following are done the offer will be considered revoked and you must return the deposit to the buyers:

1. You, the seller, sign the acceptance.
2. You deliver the signed copy of the contract to buyers or to the person authorized by buyers to receive it either in person or by mail.

Acceptance

If a real estate professional is involved in this transaction, that professional should fill out the contract.

Now that you have read and studied the purchase contract, you are ready to understand its implications. Such implications include the contingencies and the amount of money you expect to make from the sale of your home, which are the subjects of Chapter 11, "Understand Contract Implications."

Step 3: Understand Additional Terms and Conditions

The original purpose of inspections was to protect property buyers. Sellers now order inspections more often because inspection reports can convince buyers that you have nothing to hide and also provide proof of disclosure often required by law. If one is not performed previous to the signing of the purchase contract, then several options exist:

- Whoever requested the inspection hires the inspector.
- You cooperate by arranging for an inspector to enter the necessary areas within a reasonable length of time.
- If inspectors' reports disclose conditions or facts unacceptable to buyers that you are unwilling or unable to correct, buyers may cancel this agreement.

Although buyers may cancel, you and buyers may also negotiate who pays for which repairs, *or* you may reduce the price to buyers to account for some or all needed repairs. Some lenders may require that the amount of the price reduction be used to make the repairs before they allow escrow to close.

Completing Item 1: Physical and Geological Inspections

A *physical inspection* is an examination of the general physical condition of a property's site and structures. Inspection includes but is not limited to items listed. Consider having an inspection even if your state law does not require it, if you have not already done so.

A *geological inspection* is an investigation by a soils engineer for potential geological problems. This inspection is generally done only if a problem is expected or physical inspection shows a condition that requires more evaluation.

Providing a physical inspection report to buyers before you negotiate can prevent some items from becoming contingencies. Items buyers question if no inspection is done often become points to negotiate if you provide an inspection report. If buyers do not require a physical inspection, consider requesting and paying for one yourself. A physical inspection:

- Provides an excellent source of information for a real estate transfer disclosure form.
- Protects you from charges of trying to hide problems or potential problems, when you provide it to buyers in addition to a real estate transfer disclosure statement.
- Is generally less expensive than becoming involved in a lawsuit.

At their own expense, buyers may choose qualified professionals to inspect the property including but not limited to the listed aspects. Buyers agree to the following arising from the inspections:

- Keep property free and clear of any liens.
- Hold you harmless from all liability, claims, demands, damages, or costs.
- Repair all damages to the property resulting from the inspections.

For both physical and geological inspections, within 30 days after you accept the buyers' offer, buyers may:

- Write a list of problems that they claim to be defects in the condition of the property, which make it less usable for the purpose for which it is presently used or for which the property legally could be used.
- Support the list of problems with written reports.
- Deliver the list of problems and written reports to you.

Buyers may cancel this contract *if* they are not satisfied by data or conditions revealed by the reports *and* you are unwilling or unable to correct the problems.

Completing Item 2: Pest Control

Pest control inspections, sometimes called *structural pest control inspections* or *termite inspections,* are checks for other infestations or infections by other wood-destroying organisms in addition to termites. Most lenders require pest control inspections and reports. Some buyers may require this inspection even if a lender does not.

Time Limit. Within 30 days from the date you accept the buyers' offer is usually enough time for you to provide buyers with a current written pest control report.

Licensed Structural Pest Control Operators. Consider consulting your lender, title representative, or escrow officer for names of honest and competent structural pest control operators.

Completing Item 3: Energy Conservation Retrofit

Energy conservation retrofit laws may require that property comply with local minimum energy conservation standards before property can be sold or title transferred. Consult your lender, title representative, or escrow officer to determine whether your home is situated in an area where an energy conservation retrofit is required.

Compliance and Payment. The party that complies and pays is negotiable. You generally both comply with and pay for the requirements. If you must pay for the retrofit, in places where the law permits you may pay the bill by authorizing escrow to give enough credit to buyers to cover the costs of the retrofit.

Completing Item 4: Flood Hazard Area Disclosure

This disclosure informs buyers that property is located in a region designated as a *Special Flood Hazard Area.* Legally, for lenders to make a loan they must require flood insurance on a property or item attached to the property located within the zone *and* used as security for a loan.

Consult your lender, title representative, escrow officer, or insurance carrier for information whether your home is in an area where Flood Hazard Area Disclosure is required and have him or her inform you of the amount of insurance required.

Completing Item 5: Home Protection Plan

A home protection plan or home warranty ensures that specified items, such as plumbing, wiring, and major appliances, are in working order for a specified length of time. You can purchase coverage separately for other home items, such as pools and spas. When something goes wrong with one of the covered items:

- The new homeowner usually pays for a service call.
- The plan pays for the cost of the repair.
- Labor on a repair is often guaranteed for 30 days.
- Parts are often guaranteed for 90 days.

Issuing Company. Consult your lender, title representative, or escrow officer for names of providers of home protection plans:

1. Contact providers and obtain several sample policies.
2. Compare all policies carefully.
3. Choose a policy that insures all home components you wish to cover.

Payment. The party that pays is negotiable. Traditionally, either you pay or the costs are split evenly between you and buyers.

Completing Item 6: Condominium/PUD

Condominiums and planned unit developments (PUDs) are often subject to additional designations, fees, and regulations.

- *Condominium* is defined as an undivided ownership in common in a portion of a piece of real property (real estate) plus a separate interest in space in a building.
- *Planned unit development* is defined as a subdivision in which the lots are separately owned, but other areas, such as green belts and recreation facilities, are owned in common.

As soon as practical you must:

1. Provide buyers with copies of several documents:
   a. Covenants, conditions, and restrictions (CC&Rs).
   b. Articles of incorporation, the basic document filed with the correct government agency when an association incorporates.
   c. Current rules and regulations.
   d. Most recent financial statement, the report summarizing the financial condition of the homeowner's association for a specified period.
   e. Any other documents required by law.
2. Disclose to buyers in writing the following, if known:
   a. Special assessments or taxes charged on a property for benefits given to that property.
   b. Claims or demands for money or property.
   c. Litigation, lawsuits.

Time Limit. Ten calendar days from the date buyers receive the listed documents from you is usually ample time to review documents and cancel this contract by notifying you if documents disclose information or conditions buyers find unsatisfactory.

Completing Item 7: Liquidated Damages

Liquidated damages consists of the money you may keep if buyers default or breach the contract. Defaults include failing to make a good-faith effort to remove contingencies or welshing on the contract for no reason. If buyers default and fail to complete the purchase, you are not obligated to sell the property to them *or* you may sue buyers for specific performance (to carry out their agreement).

Funds deposited in escrow or trust accounts are not automatically released if you and buyers disagree. Usually, both you and buyers must give written consent or there must be a judgment before escrow releases funds.

Completing Item 8: Dispute Arbitration

Arbitration is taking a controversy to an unbiased third person who issues a decision after a hearing at which you both may speak. If arbitration is binding, you both agree to abide by the person's decision. Consider opting for arbitration in most cases. Arbitration is almost always faster and less costly than a court of law. You cannot normally appeal an arbitrator's decision to another arbitrator or a court of law.

Clauses in a contract may provide that you and buyers:

- Agree to neutral arbitration of all applicable disputes.
- Give up your right to court trial about these disputes.
- Affect your legal rights to discovery (disclosure of things previously unknown) and appeal (resort to a higher court to review the decision of a lower court).
- Admit you voluntarily agreed to the arbitration clause.

11

Understand Contract Implications

Understanding implications of any contract can help you negotiate the best contract. Implications for real estate sales contracts can include the amount of proceeds you expect to receive, the contingencies you decide to allow, and the taxes you expect to pay.

Step 1: Understand Monetary Implications

To understand the monetary implications of any sales contract, calculate the expected results.

Estimate of Proceeds Worksheet—Working

To estimate the amount you will receive from selling your home, collect the following documents to use as you prepare the Estimate of Proceeds Worksheet—Working:

- Purchase contract buyers submitted to you.
- Estimate of Proceeds Worksheet—Preliminary that you completed in preparing for the negotiations. See Chapter 9, "Prepare for Negotiation."
- If you did not prepare the Estimate of Proceeds Worksheet—Preliminary, you may fill out the Estimate of Proceeds Worksheet—Working using the instructions here, starting with step 2.
    1. Using a copy of the Estimate of Proceeds Worksheet from Chapter 9, place an *X* in the box marked Working.

2. If the purchase contract lists a specific amount for an item for which you will pay, use that amount.

3. Where the purchase contract lists no specific amount for an item for which you will pay, use the estimate you entered on the Estimate of Proceeds Worksheet—Preliminary.

4. If you did not list the item on the preliminary estimate or did not prepare a preliminary estimate, check the source of cost information listed in Chapter 9, "Prepare for Negotiation," for the approximate cost of this item.

Other Monetary Implications

Understand that you may be charged for an item even though you do not list it. If you do not list who will pay the charge in the purchase contract, escrow generally assigns these costs according to local customs.

Step 2: Understand Contingencies

Understanding *contingencies*—the conditions on which a valid contract depends—is vital. It allows you to know which conditions will work for you and how to handle these conditions.

Contingency Basics

A contingency provides that both you and buyers are released from all duties of the contract if a condition on which the contract depends fails to occur. A typical home purchase contract contains many of these conditions. Before you sell, consider how you want to deal with various contingencies that may occur. Such planning can aid you greatly in your sale.

Preventing Contingencies

When you offer your home for sale, act to prevent contingencies, if possible:

1. Give potential buyers copies of a disclosure statement and any inspections performed on the property.

2. Attempt to reach an agreement on each item that contains no contingencies. Giving a little in the negotiation now may save you time, worry, and money later.

3. Use a contingency only if you are not able to reach an agreement.

4. Use specific and definite wording in all contracts you prepare, so you and the buyers have no misunderstandings.

5. Ask buyers to sign a statement that they will act in good faith to remove contingencies as soon as possible by obtaining whatever information, approval, or inspections are necessary.

6. Use a conditions release clause for the contingencies you specify in addition to the regular purchase contract.

Condition(s) Release

Understand that a condition(s) release provides that:

- You will continue to market your home until one of the following occurs:
  ○ You receive another offer that does not contain the contingencies you and the buyers agreed on.
  ○ Buyers remove the contingencies.
- If you receive another contract without the contingencies you specified, both of the following apply:
  ○ Buyers have the amount of time you agree on in hours or days to remove the contingencies.
  ○ If the buyers do not remove the contingencies, you may sell your home to the persons who offered you the contract without the contingencies.

Many variations of the condition(s) release form exist. We present a generic form in Section VI, "Worksheets and Contracts." Check your state's version of this form against the descriptions of items in this section.

As the form notes, you have the right to continue to offer your property for sale.

Time Limit

If buyers fail to remove the contingencies within the time limit listed in the addendum:

1. The real estate purchase contract, as well as this contract, shall end and have no effect.

2. You must return the buyers' deposit.

Receipt of Notice

The Notice to Buyer to Remove Condition(s) in Section VI, "Worksheets and Contracts," is considered received by buyers when it meets the listed requirements. In this case, that is when either buyers or their agent receives delivery of this notice in person or by certified mail, *and* the notice is addressed as listed.

Step 3: Understand How to Handle Contingencies

You can take several steps to manage the contingencies that you negotiated into your contract. Use a copy of the Conditions Worksheet—Working in Section VI, "Worksheets and Contracts," to keep track of the contingencies in the contract and how they are handled.

1. Use your copy of the purchase contract as a reference.
2. Mark an *X* in the box marked Working.
3. Mark an *X* for the conditions that apply in the Used column.
4. Enter information regarding the checked conditions.
5. As each contingency is met, insert an *X* in the Met column.
6. Be sure that you act in good faith to remove contingencies as soon as possible by obtaining whatever information, approval, or inspections are necessary.
7. Have buyers sign a condition(s) release form for each contingency as soon as that condition is met.
8. Realize that if a contingency in a contract is not met for any reason the contract is canceled *unless* you and buyers choose to negotiate a modification of the condition.

After you have acted to prevent contingencies or, if necessary, removed contingencies and obtained statements from the buyers that they have been removed, you are ready to understand other possible offers you may receive on your property. These offers include leases, options, or lease options. They may be used alone or in combination with each other. They may also be used with purchase agreements.

12
Understand Other Possible Offers

Buyers and sellers often use agreements in addition to, in combination with, or instead of the purchase offer. For example, you may lease your property to buyers before closing, buyers may lease the property to you after closing, buyers may lease your property with an option to buy, or you may give buyers an option to purchase only.

Step 1: Learn about Basic Contracts

Leases and options are the basic real estate contracts you may encounter in addition to purchase contracts.

Lease

A *lease* is a contract by which one party (lessor) transfers possession and use of property for a limited, designated term at a specified price and under the stipulated conditions to another party (lessee).

You can buy blank lease forms at your local stationery store or in some states from your Board of Realtors. Books available at your local library or bookstore contain sample leases. Consult with your attorney or real estate professional if you have questions concerning leasing. Also consider consulting your accountant or tax preparer to calculate your estimated tax consequences during the period you plan to lease the property.

ADVANTAGES
- Enables you to obtain income from a property that otherwise might be costing you money.

113

- You may feel free to move into another home if you know the home you are selling can be rented.

DISADVANTAGES

- Lessees may cause considerable damage before you can remove them.
- Lessees can be difficult to remove at times if there is a problem.

Option

An option is a contract that gives potential buyers (optionees) the *right* to purchase a property before the specified future date for the amount and under the conditions listed in the contract. Also, buyers agree to pay an added amount—an option fee—if they do not use the option.

ADVANTAGE

- If buyers do not use the option, they pay you an option fee.

DISADVANTAGES

- You may worry about whether the persons to whom you gave the option will purchase your home.
- Buyers can decide to purchase your property at any time within the lease period.
- You do not receive money for the sale until the property is sold, usually near or at the end of the lease period.
- Unless you negotiate otherwise, you cannot legally raise the property's price during the term of the contract.

If you use an option, consider:

1. Using an attorney to draw up the agreements because of their complex nature.
2. Having buyers make a deposit toward a down payment.
3. Making the return of the deposit to the optionees contingent on your later successful sale of the property to other buyers.
4. Negotiating that the price of the property when the buyers exercise the option be a value to be determined by some mutually acceptable method.

Step 2: Learn about Other Contracts

In selling your home, you may also encounter combination contracts, including lease purchase and sale leaseback agreements, as well as lease and purchase options.

Lease Purchase Agreements

If you lease your property *to* buyers during the period *before* escrow closes, use a lease in combination with the purchase contract or a consolidated form, such as an Interim Occupancy Agreement.

ADVANTAGES

- You may feel free to move into another home if you know the home you are selling can be rented.
- You receive income from your property, which otherwise might be a drain on your cash flow.

DISADVANTAGES

- Buyers may see things about your home that they do not like and refuse to complete the sale.
- You may have difficulty getting buyers to vacate the property if they refuse to go through with the sale.
- Buyers who refuse to complete the sale might cause considerable damage before you can remove them.

Sale Leaseback Agreements

If you rent or lease your former home *from* buyers *after* escrow closes, use a lease in combination with a purchase contract or a specific sale leaseback form, such as an Interim Occupancy Agreement.

ADVANTAGES

- You may not have to bother moving more than once.
- After closing the sale, you will be in a better financial position to buy another home.

DISADVANTAGE

- You must move out of the home by the date you negotiate. If the escrow on your new home does not close on time, you may have no place to live.

Lease Option

If you agree to lease your property with an option to buy, use a lease option or a combination of a lease, an option, and a purchase contract.

ADVANTAGES

- Enables you to obtain income from a property that otherwise might be costing you money.
- If buyers do not use the option, they pay you an option fee.

DISADVANTAGES

- You may worry about whether the persons to whom you gave the option will purchase your home.

- Buyers can decide to purchase your property at any time within the lease period.
- You do not receive money for the sale until the property is sold, usually near or at the end of the lease period.
- Unless you negotiate otherwise, you cannot legally increase the property price during the contract.
- After buyers live in the property, they may discover certain inconveniences that they did not expect and may try to avoid purchasing the property.

If you decide to use a lease option, consider:

1. Requesting approval for the lease option from the lender.
2. Including a provision for buyers to forfeit the deposit if they decide not to purchase the property on a lease option.
3. Adding a clause that buyers make monthly lease payments to equal or exceed payments on the existing loan.
4. Inserting a provision that you credit buyers with a portion of the monthly lease payment toward the purchase price.
5. Calculating your estimated tax consequences during the period that you plan to lease the property.

Purchase Option

The purchase option contract states that potential buyers have the *right* to purchase the property before the specified future date for the amount listed and under the conditions specified in the contract. Also, they agree to pay an option fee that is applied to the purchase price if they use the option or is forfeited if they do not. If you agree to grant a purchase option, use a purchase option form or a combination option and purchase contract.

ADVANTAGES
- You may have sold your home and may not have to worry about marketing it any longer.
- You will receive some cash—the option fee—even if the sale is not completed.

DISADVANTAGES
- You may worry about whether the persons to whom you gave the option will purchase your home.
- Buyers can decide to purchase your property at any time within the option period.
- You do not receive money until the property is sold, usually near or at the end of the option period.

- You cannot increase the price for your property during the term of the contract. A price increase is illegal even if all other properties in the area increase substantially in value.

Step 3: Learn about Backup Offers

Backup offers are offers that you accept in a secondary position to the offer you accepted previously. You may want to accept backup offers because of the possibility that a contract may become void in some way. Voiding can occur because contingencies in the primary purchase agreement are not satisfied or some other complication occurs (see Chapter 15, "Handle Closing Complications"). When the first offer fails, the next offer in line automatically becomes the primary offer. If you decide you want to accept backup offers, consider:

- Telling the buyers from whom you accept the primary offer that you plan to accept backup offers.
- Negotiating backup offers in the same way you negotiated the primary purchase offer.
- Including a clause noting that it is a backup offer and as such is subject to the nonperformance of any previous offers.
- Including a statement allowing buyers to withdraw a backup offer in writing at any time before you notify them that their offer is in first position.
- Numbering each backup offer as you accept it to avoid priority disputes.
- Telling all the other offerers, including the buyers, when you accept another backup offer.

After you study the types of other offers you may encounter, you are now ready to learn about, and perhaps make, a counteroffer.

13

Handle Counteroffers

You will probably receive offers for your property that do not satisfy your expectations in such areas as price, financing, inspections, or occupancy. Making an offer of your own (counteroffering) indicates to buyers that you:

- Are not willing to accept the offer as written.
- Are motivated to sell your home.
- Are willing to negotiate.
- Desire different terms in the places you have made changes.

Step 1: Prepare for Counteroffers

Few sellers receive exactly the terms they ask for on the first offer. If you understand at the beginning that you are likely to write a counteroffer, you will probably find the process of counteroffering easier.

Estimate of Proceeds Worksheet—Counteroffer

Estimate the amount you will receive from the sale of your home as modified by the counteroffer:

1. Make a copy of your Estimate of Proceeds Worksheet—Preliminary Section VI, "Worksheets and Contracts."
2. Check the box preceding Counteroffer at the top of the worksheet.
3. Gather documents necessary to prepare the Estimate of Proceeds Worksheet—Counteroffer, including the:

    a. Counteroffer you are preparing.

    b. Latest purchase offer buyers presented to you.

    c. Estimate of Proceeds Worksheet—Working that you previously prepared.

If you have not prepared the Estimate of Proceeds Worksheet—Working, prepare the Estimate of Proceeds Worksheet—Counteroffer, in Section VI, "Worksheets and Contracts," using the instructions provided in Chapter 9, as well as those provided in this chapter.

4. Insert an *X* in front of the word *Counteroffer* on a copy of the Estimate of Proceeds Worksheet and fill in the requested information.

5. List on the worksheet the amount of each charge for the items that you intend to pay. Use the amount from the most current available document. Use an amount from an earlier document only if that is the most current information available.

6. If the item is not listed on any of the documents, check the source of information shown in Chapter 9 for the approximate cost of this item.

7. Understand that for any charges you do not itemize, escrow will generally assign a payer of these charges in agreement with local customs.

Conditions Worksheet—Counteroffer

Prepare the Counteroffer Conditions Worksheet in Section VI, "Worksheets and Contracts," so that you understand exactly what contingencies apply.

1. Make a copy of the Conditions Worksheet.
2. Mark an *X* in front of the word *Counteroffer* on the Conditions Worksheet, then fill in the requested information.

Step 2: Understand Counteroffers

If your changes are relatively simple and few in number, use a form similar to the counteroffer form. Many variations of this form exist. We present a generic form in Section VI, "Worksheets and Contracts."

Changes or Amendments

Consider entering the changes or amendments by:

1. Listing sections and changes in the order in which they appear in your real estate purchase contract. In this way the counteroffer may be most easily understood. Legally, changes and amendments may be made in any order.

2. Writing the section number and letter designation, as well as the section caption. Designations and captions:
   - Are most easily understood if listed in the same order as those in the real estate purchase contract you want to change.
   - Make sections of the agreement easier to locate.
   - Are not intended to be part of the contract.
3. Write the changes and amendments you want to make for the section you listed. Be definite and specific.

Until you receive a copy of this counteroffer accepted and signed by buyers, you have the right to:

1. Continue to market the property described in this contract for sale.
2. Accept any offer that is acceptable to you.

Seller

All persons holding title must sign this contract, unless one person has power of attorney for another.

Step 3: Understand Counteroffer Logistics

Understanding the logistics of counteroffers can aid you in handling them more effectively.

Writing a Counteroffer

When you make a counteroffer, be aware of several points:

1. The counteroffer must be in writing. Like offers, counteroffers are not valid unless written.
2. The length of time buyers have to accept your counteroffer should be stated clearly. Sellers usually offer an acceptance time ranging from several hours to several days.

Revoking a Counteroffer

You may revoke your counteroffer any time before buyers accept your counteroffer *and* communicate their acceptance of your counteroffer in writing.

Accepting Another Purchase Offer

You may accept another offer as long as buyers to whom you made a counteroffer have not accepted the counteroffer.

Buyers Accepting Your Counteroffer

Understand that to establish a binding legal contract, buyers must accept and communicate their acceptance according to several guidelines:

- In writing.
- Within the time limits allowed by your counteroffer.
- Before you revoke the counteroffer.

Timing

You and the buyers may continue to make as many counteroffers as you wish, until you agree on the terms or decide to discontinue the process. When you and buyers continue to make offers and counteroffers, consider:

1. Making or accepting from buyers only *written* offers or counteroffers.
2. Stating clearly the length of time buyers have to accept your counteroffer.
3. Choosing the form to use depending on the changes involved:
   - Use a counteroffer form to make counteroffers for which the changes are relatively few and simple.
   - Write a counteroffer using a real estate purchase contract for changes that are numerous or complex.
4. You may revoke your counteroffer any time (within the time limits specified in the contract) before buyers accept your counteroffer *and* communicate their acceptance.
5. Buyers may also revoke their offer any time (within the time limits specified in the contract) before you accept their offer *and* communicate your acceptance.

After completing the negotiation process—including possible counteroffers and signing a written real estate purchase contract to sell your home—you are ready to learn about and prepare for closing.

SECTION IV
Close

14

Understand Closing Basics

Closing or settlement is the process in which funds and property title are transferred between you and the buyers. Although closing could be accomplished by you and buyers simply getting together and exchanging money and documents, most property transactions today use an escrow type of closing.

Step 1: Understand Escrow

Escrow is a type of closing by which you and buyers deposit money and/or documents with a neutral third party. You and buyers give the third party instructions to hold and disburse documents and funds after certain conditions are met. Whoever handles the closing acts as an agent for both you and buyers. This person is often referred to as the *escrow holder.*

ADVANTAGES
Consider having an escrow because of the complexity of the closing process. The advantages of escrow are that a neutral third party is responsible for:

- Keeping documents and funds safe.
- Making computations.
- Receiving and distributing funds.
- Drawing up, acquiring, and recording documents.
- Carrying out any other terms of the contract.

- Determining that all conditions have been satisfied.
- Ensuring that buyers receive the appropriate documents.
- Ensuring that you receive the appropriate funds.
- Providing an accounting for the transfer process.
- Complying with federal, state, and local tax regulations.

DISADVANTAGE

The slight cost involved in having an escrow.

Functions of Escrow

Following is a short list of the functions that escrow holders often perform while they act as impartial stake holders and communicate with everyone involved about the transaction. Escrow holders have certain responsibilities:

- Preparing escrow instructions.
- Preparing and assembling relevant documents.
- Obtaining signatures.
- Proceeding with title search by:
  1. Requesting the title search.
  2. Receiving and reviewing preliminary title report to determine what actions to take to conform to the condition of title required in the escrow instructions.
  3. Requesting demands (demand for payoff) from lenders, if you desire to pay off existing loans.
  4. Requesting an explanation of liens against the property as listed on the preliminary title report.
  5. Analyzing taxes on the report to be sure terms are correct and conform to the escrow instructions.
  6. Receiving demands from lenders.
  7. Entering demands from lenders into the file.
- Proceeding to process a new loan, if any, concurrently with the title search by:
  1. Requesting or preparing a new loan application.
  2. Obtaining a loan approval in the form of a loan commitment letter from the lender.
  3. Examining approved loans to be sure that terms are correct and conform to escrow instructions.
  4. Requesting loan documents.
- Proceeding with a loan takeover (assumption), if any, concurrently with the title search and the processing of a new loan (if applicable) by:
  1. Requesting from lenders beneficiary statements giving transfer terms and payment status for each loan.
  2. Receiving and reviewing each beneficiary statement.

3. Entering each beneficiary statement into the file.
4. Reviewing each loan's transfer terms and payment status to determine whether approval is necessary to record.

- Reviewing the file to determine that all:
  1. Conditions have been met.
  2. Documents are drawn (prepared).
  3. Documentation is correct.
  4. Documents are available for signatures.
- If the file is complete, proceeding by:
  1. Calculating costs.
  2. Requesting signatures on all unsigned documents.
- Complete the closing by:
  1. Sending documents to the title company.
  2. Requesting and obtaining funds from the buyers.
  3. Returning loan documents (usually the note, signed disclosure statements, and instructions) to lender.
- Funding the loan (requesting and obtaining loan funds from lender).
- Requesting recording (official entry of transactions, liens, satisfaction of mortgages, and reconveyances into the permanent record of a county).
- Closing the file.
- Preparing buyers' and seller's closing statements.
- Disbursing distributing funds.
- Completing the closing.
- Sending final documents to all interested parties (seller, buyers, and lender).
- Preparing federal, state, and local tax documents (1099s, FIRPTAs, deed tax stamps, and so on).

Lenders usually require escrow as a condition of making a loan. Some states require escrow for the sale of houses only or in cases such as court sales—including public administration and probate sales. Check with lenders or escrow companies to determine whether escrow on your home is required by law.

Because of the complexity of the process involved, having an escrow holder can do much to protect you when you sell your home.

Actions Prohibited for Escrow Holders

Escrow holders are usually prohibited from doing the following:

- Offering advice.
- Negotiating with you and buyers.
- Revealing information about the escrow to persons who are not a party to the transaction.

- Preparing or revising escrow instructions without the authorization of you *and* the buyers.

Requirements of a Valid Escrow

A valid escrow arrangement is a legal and binding written contract between buyers and seller. Requirements for a legal and binding contract include factors described here.

Competency of Buyers and Seller

To be competent, you and the buyers must meet certain requirements set by your state. You and the buyers often must:

- Be natural persons (not corporations) who meet all the following criteria:
  - Adult (at least a minimum age set by your state laws) or emancipated minors (state laws vary but often include being lawfully married or divorced, on duty in the armed forces, or emancipated by court order).
  - Mentally competent.
  - Not a felon deprived of civil rights.
- Be artificial persons, such as corporations, partnerships, or a joint venture. Individuals from such entities who sign documents must have the authority to act as a representative of the entity.
- Have a legal right (such as power of attorney) to enter into contracts involving the property.

Consideration

Consideration is anything of value that influences a person to enter into a contract, such as money, a deed, a service, an item of personal property, an act (including the payment of money), or a promise (including the promise to pay on a loan).

If consideration is an act or service, that act or service must be performed *after* you and the buyers enter into the contract.

Lawful Object

To be legally enforceable, the promises and the consideration must be legal.

Mutual Agreement

There must be agreement between you and the buyers about the wording and conditions.

Selection of an Escrow Holder

Depending on the area, the party that acts as escrow holder can include independent escrow companies, title companies, escrow departments of lending institutions (banks, savings and loans, and so on), attorneys, and real estate brokers.

Consider choosing an escrow holder who is willing to take the time to explain to you what is happening and what you need to do and is located within a convenient distance from your current residence so you can deliver and sign documents easily.

Timing of Selection

Select an escrow holder during this period of preparation for closing if you have not already done so.

Step 2: Establish an Escrow

To set up an escrow account, you must open the escrow and provide the escrow holder with information for the escrow instructions.

Opening an Escrow

After you select an escrow holder, open the escrow by following these steps:

1. Contact the escrow holder by telephone or in person.
2. Give the escrow holder all of the relevant information regarding the sale.
3. Deposit the buyers' earnest money with the escrow holder, preferably in person *or* if necessary by certified mail.

Providing Take Sheet Information

The escrow officer collects information necessary to prepare escrow instructions on a form called a "take sheet." Data the escrow holder may need to prepare escrow instructions are described in the following sections.

Property Description

From your deed or title insurance policy, the property description includes:

- Property address.
- Legal description.
- Type of property.

Parties to the Transaction

From the purchase contract, the list of parties includes:

- Your name, address, and telephone number.
- Buyers' names, addresses, and telephone numbers.

Escrow Information

From the purchase contract, the escrow information includes:

- Time period.
- Proposed closing date.

Sales Price

From the purchase contract, the sales price lists:

- Amount.
- Terms.

Loans Currently on the Property

From your payment statement or lender, loan information includes data about mortgages, trust deeds, and home equity lines of credit, specifically the following:

- Loan number, amount, and rate of interest.
- Amount of monthly principal and interest payments.
- Lender's name, address, and telephone number.

Loans Buyers Want to Put on the Property

From the purchase contract, buyers' loan information includes data regarding:

- Loan amount and rate of interest.
- Amount of monthly principal and interest payments.
- Lender's name, address, and telephone number.
- Proposed beginning and due dates of the loan.
- Existence or absence of an acceleration clause in the loan.
- Whether buyers requested notice of delinquency of payment.
- Amount of the loan fee.

Vesting of the Title

How the title is to be vested when the property is transferred can be obtained from the purchase contract.

Conditions of the Title

Title conditions are specified in the purchase contract and include conditions, covenants, and restrictions.

Buyers' and Seller's Costs

Information regarding who pays which costs can be obtained from the purchase contract. Unless you have specified otherwise in the documents you submit to escrow, the escrow holder usually writes escrow instructions designating costs based on local custom. You and buyers may agree on any division that does not conflict with legal requirements in your state and area. Be sure you and buyers:

1. Reach an agreement about each possible cost.
2. Communicate your agreement to the escrow officer.

Rental Information

If the property is being rented or leased, provide current information regarding names of tenants along with their rental amounts, payment dates, and security deposits.

Escrow Instructions

Escrow instructions are the written agreement between you and buyers that translates the contract into a form used by the escrow holder to conduct and close the escrow.

Understand Escrow Instructions

The escrow holder attempts to prepare escrow instructions, using the take sheet as a guideline, so that the intent and conditions are identical to those in the purchase agreement. The escrow holder then asks you and buyers to read and sign the escrow instructions. Consider taking several precautionary actions:

1. Reading the escrow instructions carefully.
2. Being sure that the intent and conditions of escrow instructions are identical to those in the purchase contract.
3. Asking questions about items you do not understand or ones that do not appear to match those in the purchase contract.
4. Signing escrow instructions *only* when you are satisfied that all items reflect *exactly* the terms of the purchase contract.

Amending Escrow Instructions

You and buyers can make amendments (changes) only when you both agree to the amendments. To amend any escrow instruction:

1. Discuss the change with buyers.
2. Obtain the buyers' agreement to the change.
3. Request that the escrow holder prepare documents for the change.
4. Request that documents containing the change be sent to both you and the buyers.
5. Sign documents authorizing the change. (The buyers must also sign to authorize the change.)
6. Return the documents to escrow. (If the documents were signed in counterparts, all counterparts signed by buyer and seller must be returned to escrow holder by both buyer and seller.)

Step 3: Handle Escrow Responsibilities

Both you and the buyers have responsibilities for completing some items in the escrow process. The steps you will be asked to take and the order in which you are asked to take them vary depending on the details of your sale, requirements of your state, usual procedure in your area, and process the escrow company uses. Ask your escrow holder to inform you and the buyers what each of you should do and when you should do it.

After you have established the escrow and understand the basics of the escrow process, you are ready to address any complications that may arise as a result of that escrow.

15

Handle Closing Complications

You, the buyers, or circumstances beyond the control of either may create complications you must resolve in order to close the sale of your property. Such complications might include:

- Your acceptance of another offer on your home when you have used a kick-out provision in your real estate purchase contract.
- Your and buyers' agreement to changes in the contract.
- Breach of contract.
- Destruction of your property.
- Disputes with buyers.

Step 1: Remove Contingencies

To prevent contingencies from becoming major difficulties:

1. Make a good-faith attempt to meet the requirements of the contingencies for which you are responsible as soon as possible. Obtain required information, approvals, and/or inspections and make required repairs. Buyers may be prone to take legal action if you do not make a good-faith attempt.
2. Cooperate with people hired by the buyers. These people include persons who need information and those who must gain access to your property.
3. Request that buyers sign a separate copy of a Condition(s) Release (found in Section VI, "Worksheets and Contracts") for each condition listed in the purchase contract, as each separate condition is met.

Step 2: Handle Unmet Conditions

If a contingency for which you or buyers are responsible is not met for any reason, the contract is over. Why it was not met may be important in influencing your action.

Renegotiate

Renegotiation could be the least expensive option, especially if you extend only the time limits for meeting conditions that have a high likelihood of being met. Consider renegotiating your present contract if:

- Buyers made what you consider a good-faith attempt but were unable to meet the terms of the conditions within the time limits on which you agreed.
- Buyers still want to purchase your property.
- You feel buyers *will* be able to meet the terms of the conditions within a period acceptable to you both.

If you decide to renegotiate, choose the type of form for the written contract, depending on the number and nature of the changes. Use a new purchase contract for numerous or major changes.

Contract Changes and Additions

Make uncomplicated and/or minor additions or deletions to the purchase contract using a Contract Changes and Additions form in Section VI, "Worksheets and Contracts."

Many variations of the contract exist. The spaces to be filled in on this form are largely self-explanatory.

Consider listing the section number and designation for each change or addition before you list the terms or conditions. Section numbers and designations make the items easier to locate in the contract.

Distribute copies of forms containing any modifications to buyers, escrow holder, and your attorneys.

Remarket

Remarketing may take a substantial amount of time and expense, depending on how long it takes you to find buyers and the length of closing involved. Remarketing may cost significantly less than dealing with buyers who try to win concessions from you. Consider remarketing your property and selling it to other buyers if you believe buyers:

- Will not be able to meet contingencies in a manner acceptable to you for any reason.
- Have not made what you consider a good-faith effort to meet contingencies but are still interested in buying your home.

- Seem to have slowed the closing process, especially if they are aware that you have certain time or money limitations.

Step 3: Accept an Offer without Conditions

Whether you can legally accept another offer without the conditions from different buyers depends on whether you have used a conditions release form or a similar agreement when you signed the purchase contract.

Conditions Release

See Section VI, "Worksheets and Contracts," for copies of the form. Conditions releases supply wipe-out or kick-out provisions to your purchase contract for those conditions you specify to be the buyer's responsibility. They provide that you will continue to market your home until one of the following occurs:

- Buyers remove those conditions you have indicated.
- You receive another offer to purchase your home that does not contain the conditions you specified. Buyers then have the amount of time you agreed on to remove the conditions. If the buyers fail to remove the conditions, you may sell your home to the persons who offered you the contract without the conditions.

Consider basing your actions on whether you signed a conditions release when you signed the purchase contract:

- If you have *not* used a conditions release form or a similar contract, do *not* accept another offer. Accepting another offer opens you to possible legal action.
- If you used a conditions release form or a similar contract to supply a wipe-out or kick-out provision, you may continue to market your property.
    1. You may continue to market until you accept another offer to buy your home that does not contain any of the conditions you specified.
    2. Inform the first buyers:
        a. You accepted another offer.
        b. They have the time agreed on in the conditions release in which to remove the specified conditions.

Conditions Removal Requests

Consider using the Notice to Buyers to Remove Conditions in Section VI, "Worksheets and Contracts," to notify buyers to remove the conditions agreed on in a conditions release form. This form serves as official notice to buyers that you have accepted another written offer. Many variations of this form exist.

The first buyers have the amount of time you both agreed to in the purchase contract to sign a firm agreement without the specified conditions. One way to sign a firm contract without the specified conditions is to have buyers sign a Notice to Buyers to Remove Conditions form.

If buyers fail to remove the conditions within the time limit given, by signing a Notice to Buyers to Remove Conditions or similar form:

1. The real estate purchase contract, plus all the rights and duties under that contract, end and become invalid.
2. You return the buyers' deposit.

Notice to Buyers to Remove Conditions

Using a Notice to Buyers to Remove Conditions, buyers can remove conditions agreed on in a conditions release form. On any form of this type expect the buyers to have:

- Entered the conditions to which they voluntarily give up claim.
- Agreed to buy the property in accord with all other terms and conditions.

If the first buyers *remove* those conditions you have specified, you *must* sell your home to the first buyers.

If the first buyers *fail to remove* those conditions you specified, your contract with these buyers is voidable. After your contract with the first buyers is voided, you may then open an escrow to sell your property to the buyers who offered you a contract without those conditions.

Step 4: Handle Other Complications

A number of other complications might occur while your property is in escrow.

Revocation

Revocation is contract cancellation after a time limit expires. The cancellation is by whoever performed according to the contract when the other party did not perform according to the contract. Handle revocation in the way that helps you achieve your desired results:

- Have the escrow holder return whatever you put into escrow if you do not want to continue the sale of your house to those buyers. Both you and the buyers are entitled to the return of the documents and funds that you deposited in escrow.

- Renegotiate the contract and open another escrow if you want to continue to sell your home to those buyers. You cannot continue with the initial escrow once it is canceled.

Breach of Contract

Breach of contract means failure to perform as promised without a legal excuse (a good reason). If you file a suit for breach of contract, in most states escrow holders must retain funds and documents until cases have been decided by the courts or by arbitration. What legally might be considered a breach of contract depends on the circumstances. For answers to questions regarding breach of contract, consult your attorney. Actions that are often considered breaches of contract by courts include:

- Your refusing *without* a legitimate reason to sell your home to buyers after you have signed a valid contract. Valid reasons for your refusal might include buyers failing to apply for a loan that they need to purchase the home or not having sufficient funds to cover a check.
- Buyers refusing without a sound reason to buy your home after they have signed a valid contract with you. Valid reasons for buyers' refusal might include unsatisfactory home or pest control inspection reports, their failure to sell property on which your sale is contingent, and their failure to obtain suitable financing.

Death or Incapacity

If you or the buyers die or become incapacitated, the timing of these events determines the effect on the sale. Generally, if:

- If you die or become incompetent *before* you deliver the deed to escrow, buyers:
  - Cannot receive the title through that escrow.
  - May sue representatives of your estate for specific performance (a court order requiring a party to perform according to the terms of the contract).
  - May negotiate a new contract with your heirs and set up a new escrow.
- If you die or become incompetent *after* depositing the deed in escrow, the escrow is not revoked. Buyers may still deposit the purchase price into escrow and receive the deed if all the other terms of the escrow are met.
- If the buyer dies before you deliver the deed to escrow, the deed is void.
- If the buyer becomes mentally incapacitated before you deliver the deed to escrow, the deed is still valid.

- If the buyer dies or becomes mentally incapacitated after you deliver the deed to escrow, the escrow is not necessarily revoked.

Property Destruction

Usually, the person with whom responsibility for costs of property destruction rests depends on the circumstances:

- Buyers are responsible if they have either assumed legal title or physical possession.
- You are responsible if buyers have neither assumed legal title nor assumed physical possession.

To protect yourself in fire, flood, earthquake, or other devastating incident should destroy the property, consider keeping your hazard insurance policy in effect until the close of escrow. If the home is destroyed, you should not lose a tremendous amount of money.

Assignment by Seller

Assignment is the transferring to another of an entire property, including all rights to the property. How you assign your interest or proceeds determines whether you must obtain the consent of the assignee. The assignee is the person to whom the interest or proceeds transfer. The assignment of your interest or any portion of your interest can be:

- *Contingent on* the close of escrow. The consent of the assignee is generally not required for this type of assignment.
- *On* the close of escrow. Escrow may require the assignee's consent in this case.

Mutual Consent and Cancellation

If you and buyers both agree to cancel an escrow, you may do so. Under these circumstances, both you and buyers are entitled to the return of documents and funds you deposited.

Implications

If a real estate professional represents you in a sale in which you and the buyers mutually consent and cancel, the broker:

- Must return the deposit to the buyers.
- Is considered to have earned the commission by providing ready, willing, and able buyers who entered into the contract.
- May sue you to obtain a commission if he or she has a contract with you.

Consider protecting yourself by:

1. Seeing your attorney before you cancel a purchase contract.
2. Using a contract release form when both you and the buyers want to declare your purchase contract invalid.

Contract Release

A contract release should contain wording indicating that you and the buyers jointly release each other from any and all of the following, which each may have against the other up to the date of the release agreement:

- Claims—demands for money or property and/or rights to payments.
- Actions—suits brought in courts.
- Demands—legal rights or obligations asserted in courts.

A release should also contain instructions to the broker or escrow holder regarding the distribution of the deposit, including amounts and to whom to disburse the funds.

Disputes

The escrow holder is a neutral stakeholder and therefore is not the proper person to make decisions in controversies between you and buyers. If you and buyers have a dispute, remember the following:

- The escrow holder usually does nothing until you and buyers resolve the situation.
- In prolonged disputes, the escrow holder sometimes initiates a court interpleader action requesting that a court take custody of deposited funds and make a judgment as to their disbursement.
- Consider consulting an attorney if you feel you and buyers have a binding contract and you have a dispute about anything other than a simple default (failure of a person to fulfill an obligation or perform a duty). An attorney may aid you in resolving the dispute without court action.
- If you and the buyers have agreed to arbitration:
  - Your controversy is to be heard by a disinterested person who will give you both a chance to speak and then make a decision on the case.
  - You must take and abide by the judgment of that person if you have agreed to binding arbitration.

Now that you have handled all the complications that have occurred before closing, you are ready for closing the sale of your house, which is the subject of Chapter 16.

16
Close!

C *losing* is the successful completion of a real estate transaction in which funds are disbursed and title is transferred from seller to buyers. To close most effectively, we suggest that you have the buyers perform a walk-through inspection, understand how escrow closes, and reconcile the closing statement.

Step 1: Perform Walk-through Inspection

A walk-through inspection is proof that you have left the property in the condition in which you agreed to leave it. Although this step is not generally legally necessary, like disclosures it provides proof that you have complied with the terms of your contract.

Understand Walk-through Inspection

A walk-through inspection, usually done by you and buyers within a few days before escrow closes, is an inspection verifying that:

- All systems and appliances are in good working order except as noted in your contract.
- You made all repairs you agreed to make.
- You replaced all items you agreed to replace.
- You have removed all your personal items from the house.
- You have left the house in the condition you agreed on with the buyers or at least swept, vacuumed, and dusted.

Prepare Walk-through Inspection Worksheet

Consider using the Walk-through Inspection Worksheet in Section VI, "Worksheets and Contracts," to conduct your walk-through inspection.

1. Fill in the heading of the worksheet.
2. If item is acceptable on inspection, have buyers write their initials in the OK column.
3. If an item needs to be fixed, have buyers write an *X* in the Fix column and write how the item needs to be fixed.
4. Write in additional items in the spaces provided.
5. Have the buyers sign a copy of the completed worksheet.
6. Obtain a copy of the completed worksheet for your records.

Step 2: Understand Closing Escrow

Understanding how the escrow transaction closes can make you comfortable with a process many buyers and sellers find very confusing. An escrow is complete when all conditions listed in the escrow instructions are met and all acts performed. When an escrow is complete, the escrow holder disburses the funds and documents to close the escrow.

Step 3: Reconcile Closing Statement

Reconciling your closing statement is much like checking an invoice for goods and services. Make sure you were charged only for items for which you agreed to pay and for the amount you agreed to pay.

To reconcile your closing statement:

1. Compare your closing statement to the appropriate Estimate of Proceeds Worksheet, that is, the last one you used to calculate your estimated proceeds.
2. If there is a significant difference between your estimate and what you were charged, check with your closing agent or escrow holder for an explanation of the discrepancy.

Congratulations for selling your home without a broker! Remember, after you close the escrow on your home, sooner or later you must handle the tax consequences of your sale. Handling your taxes is the subject of Chapter 17.

SECTION V
Wrap Up

17

Handle Taxes

Selling a home has important tax consequences. Because tax laws recently underwent—and are continuing to undergo—significant changes, consider contacting your accountant or tax preparer for more current and detailed information.

Step 1: Calculate Tax Costs

Tax laws may directly affect you when you sell your home.

New Law

The Tax Acts of 1997 and 1998 have combined to give most of us who own homes a wonderful tax break when we sell. On the surface, not much appears to have changed. Under the old law, we could sell our home and, as long as we bought another home of equal or greater value within two years, any tax we might have on the profit would be deferred. We could keep selling each home for a more expensive one every two years. Once we reached age 55, we could sell the "Ponderosa" and take the once-in-a-lifetime $125,000 exclusion on any deferred gains and pay no tax on the profits from all those home sales.

The new law says that if you are a married couple, you can exclude up to $500,000 of gain on the sale of your home, if you are single, you can exclude up to $250,000 of gain on the sale of your home. Whether you are married or single, you can do this over and over again with each new home. The only requirement is that you must have owned and lived in the home for at least two of the last five years. No once-in-a-lifetime-over-55-must-defer-the-gain malarkey.

What if you exceed the $500,000 or $250,000 thresholds? Any gains above those figures will be taxed as capital gains with a current cap of 20 percent. As you are reading this, check to see if Congress has changed anything. Be especially vigilant with regard to the retroactive features that Congress puts in tax bills. You may sell your home in June 2001 with the current tax rules in place and then have Congress change the laws in October 2001 and make those changes retroactive to January 1, 2001. That would be nothing new. Just pay attention.

Figure Your Tax

Let's apply some numbers to this discussion so you can see how these rules work when you sell your home. The key number is not the sales price. You could sell your home for $1 million and not have to pay capital gains tax. The key number is the *spread* between what you paid for your home when you bought it plus the cost of any improvements you made while you lived in it and the sales price.

What if you paid $400,000 for your home in 1997, made $75,000 worth of improvements in 1999 and were single and sold it in 2001? Up to what sales price could you receive with no tax consequences? You are correct if you said a sales price of $725,000! ($400,000 + $75,000 + $250,000 = $725,000). Assume the same scenario, except you are married. Now up to what sales price could you receive with no tax consequences? $975,000! ($400,000 + $75,000 + $500,000 = $975,000). Our tax advice to you is to get married before you sell!

Let's look at one more example with some higher numbers. You bought your home in 1997 for $1,825,000. In 1998, you made $215,000 worth of improvements. You are married. You sell your home in 2001 for $2,625,000. What is your maximum tax consequence? $1,825,000 + $215,000 + $500,000 = $2,540,000. The spread is $2,625,000 − $2,540,000 = $85,000. $85,000 × 20 percent = $17,000 in tax.

Tax-Deductible Expenses

If you itemize deductions, some of the costs of the sale of your home may be tax deductible. Check with your accountant or tax preparer for the current status of tax deductibility of marketing costs, closing costs, and moving expenses.

Marketing Costs

The costs of marketing efforts, including fix-up expenses (improvements, repairs, and attractiveness items) and advertising may be deductible from your adjusted sales price. To be deductible an item must be:

- Performed during the 90-day period before you place your property on the market.
- Paid for within 30 days after the closing date.

Closing Costs

Closing costs, such as prepaid interest, prepaid taxes, points, escrow fees, title fees, and recording fees are deductible.

Moving Costs

Moving expenses are deductible as an itemized expense on Schedule A of your federal income tax forms.

Installment Sale Imputed Interest

You may sell your home and help buyers finance the purchase price by extending them credit using a seller carry-back loan. If you receive your sales price over more than one year, in effect, you have made an installment sale. You spread your gain and thus any tax consequences over more than one tax year.

The IRS requires that you charge a minimum interest rate on seller carry-back financing. If you do not charge the minimum rate, the IRS will assign (impute) a rate the service says you should have charged. The IRS will tax you as if you had received interest at the higher rate, plus the service will penalize you for not having paid this tax earlier, for example:

- You carry back a $15,000 second loan at 6 percent interest.
- IRS minimum interest rate is 9 percent.
- Therefore, the IRS imputes a 9 percent rate on the loan you made to buyers.
- The IRS taxes you as if you had received interest at 9 percent and also charges you a penalty.

Conversion of a Principal Residence

You can convert your principal residence into rental property and vice versa. With rental property, you:

- May take repairs and maintenance expenses as deductions.
- Must take depreciation. Currently, depreciation for residential property is calculated on a 27.5-year or 40-year straight line method. Subtract depreciation from your basis.
- May take a loss on the sale.

If you convert rental property into your principal residence and then sell, you:

- May not deduct repairs and maintenance.
- Must subtract accrued depreciation from the basis in calculating your gain.
- May not take a loss on the sale.

Consult your accountant or tax preparer if either of these situations applies.

Foreign Investment in Real Property Tax Act (FIRPTA)

You may be asked to sign an affidavit stating that you are not a nonresident alien for the purposes of U.S. income taxation in order to comply with FIRPTA regulations. The Foreign Investment in Real Property Tax Act (FIRPTA) is a federal law designed to make sure that foreign nationals selling property in the United States pay capital gains tax on their profit.

Buyers may be liable to the IRS for up to 10 percent of the sales price, plus penalties and interest, if:

- Buyers are nonresident aliens for U.S. income taxation.
- No exemptions apply.
- Buyers do not deduct and withhold the required tax.

FIRPTA requires that buyers deduct and withhold 10 percent of the sales price to pay the tax unless certain exemptions apply. Exemptions are as follows:

- Buyers purchase your home to use as their personal residence and the price they paid was not more than $300,000.
- You, as seller, signed an affidavit that you are not a nonresident alien for the purposes of U.S. income taxation.
- The buyers established an exemption under IRS code.

IRS Form 1099S

Since January 1, 1987, the closing agent is required to provide you and the IRS with a completed Form 1099S entitled "Statement for Recipients of Proceeds from Real Estate Transactions." This form contains information regarding your name, address of the property sold, sales price, and closing date.

Under the new law, if all the gain qualifies for the exclusion of up to $500,000 for married people or $250,000 for single people, the seller will not receive a 1099S because there is no tax due and no need to make a report to the IRS.

Step 2: Prepare Final Tax Implications Worksheet

Use the parts of the Final Tax Implications Worksheet in Section VI, "Worksheets and Contracts," to:

1. Calculate your gain on the sale of your residence.
2. Calculate if you have a taxable gain.

Complete the worksheets to get an idea of what your tax ramifications may be. Consider checking with your accountant or tax preparer to verify your calculations and obtain more current and detailed information. Laws in this area have recently been undergoing significant changes.

Step 3: Report and Pay Taxes

After you read this chapter, understand what you need to report, and calculate the results, we recommend that you:

1. Report the results of your sale if required.
2. Pay taxes on the sale when due.

Moving is not technically considered part of selling your home, although you generally move close to the time you sell. By understanding moving and handling it effectively, you can save time and money. Moving is the subject of Chapter 18.

18

Move!

Selling your home usually requires a move. Understanding and applying certain techniques can keep money in your pocket when you move.

Step 1: Prepare for Moving

You can save money and aggravation by preparing for your move ahead of time.

Decide What to Move

Decide what you don't want to move beforehand, and then handle the preparations so that you have less to move:

1. Consume or give away excess food and beverages.
2. Sell items you do not need or use but that are worth selling.
3. Give away items you don't need or use that are not worth selling but are still usable. Get a receipt for your donation if it is tax deductible.
4. Discard items that are unusable.
5. Sell, donate, or discard heavy but relatively inexpensive items that are not cost-effective to move, including lumber, firewood, old appliances, and plants. Unless plants are rare or expensive, buying new plants after you move is cheaper and easier. Soil and pots are often heavy. Loading plants is up to the moving van driver's discretion because of potential pests.

Some states have strict rules about plant materials. Check with states in which you plan to travel.

6. Dispose of potentially hazardous substances that are always dangerous and often illegal to ship, such as:
   - Explosives, flammables, and combustibles, including propane.
   - Pressurized containers of all types.
   - Pesticides, herbicides, and other poisons.

Obtain Written Relocation Policies

Obtain written relocation policies if your employer is going to pay for part or all of the move.

Check Homeowner's Insurance

Check your homeowner's insurance to see:

- Whether your policy covers moving, including liability; cargo protection, both loss and theft; equipment damage; and medical expenses.
- Whether it contains a floater for valuable items, in addition to life insurance.
- The limits of each coverage on your policy.

Step 2: Plan Your Move

You can have a moving company move your goods, move them yourself, or use a combination of methods. Before you decide what method to use, understand what is involved with each method.

Moving Companies

By understanding what is involved with a move by professional movers, you can usually save yourself money.

Cost Factors

Moving companies base the costs of moving your goods on several factors.

Weight. Movers weigh the truck before and after your goods are loaded to determine the weight of your shipment.

Distance. Movers use charts that give the basic cost per 100 pounds. These costs are calculated for a range of weights and a range of distances.

Insurance. Movers include protection against damage and loss based on a required minimum amount per pound, *if* you request coverage. The actual value of items is usually much greater than the minimum per pound coverage. Actual value is the depreciated value of item at the present time, not full cost of replacing item.

Consider doing the following:

1. Buying higher coverage than the minimum provided. Buy coverage for at least actual value, if not the replacement value.
2. Inquiring about options for liability coverage available through the moving company.
3. Obtaining temporary coverage for the move if your homeowner's policy does not contain moving coverage.

Storage. Storage charges are based primarily on weight but may vary widely from area to area. Other charges might include a:

- Handling fee for unloading truck.
- Delivery charge for delivering goods to a new location.
- Flat access fee plus an hourly access rate for access to your goods during storage.

Delivery. Delivery is included in the price of the move during normal working hours. For weekend, holiday, or after-hours delivery at:

- Your request, movers usually add an additional charge.
- Driver's request, movers should not charge you extra.

Moving Special Items. Professional movers usually charge extra for moving certain large, heavy items, including but not limited to:

- Pianos, organs, and grandfather clocks.
- Hot tubs, Jacuzzis, spas, and whirlpool baths.
- Play houses and tool sheds.
- Automobiles, motorcycles, golf carts, and snowmobiles.
- Trailers of all types.
- Boats, unmounted campers, campers, and mini motor homes.
- Riding mowers, farm equipment, and tractors.

Other Common Charges. Other charges by professional movers may include but are not limited to:

- Providing moving containers, such as cartons.
- Packing and/or unpacking.
- Disassembly and/or assembly of items.
- Carrying items up or down flights of stairs.
- Carrying items an excessive distance.
- Pickup and/or delivery at locations other than your home.
- Extra time over estimate.

Tips. Although definitely not required, giving the movers a small tip after loading and again after unloading your belongings is a nice gesture.

Usual Moving Company Procedure

Many moving companies perform a regular estimate using these steps:

1. Estimator makes a price estimate of your move based on cost factors listed earlier.
2. Movers determine the weight of your shipment by weighing the truck before and after loading and finding the difference.
3. You pay the total charge based on shipment weight in cash or certified check *before* the driver will unload your belongings.
4. If the total amount you owe is greater than estimated total amount plus 10 percent, you pay only the estimated amount before the driver will unload the truck.
5. You pay the balance within the period the company indicates, often 30 days.

Money-Saving Ideas

You may save money when using a professional mover by:

1. Finding out which moving companies have the best reputations in your area and dealing with only these companies.
2. Calling the three top companies.
   a. Ask each company whether it takes your shipment to its destination or transfers it to another company. Transfer often means extra handling for your goods and potential extra problems for you.
   b. If the company transports your goods to its destination, ask the company to provide an estimate.
3. Letting each estimator know that you are getting several other estimates and comparing price and quality.
4. Asking the estimator to list what services are provided and to itemize the price for each service.
5. Asking whether there is a time of the year, month, or week (an off period) when you can get a lower price.
6. Asking whether the company will repay you for expenses you must pay if delivery is delayed through no fault of yours, and if so,
   a. What items are included.
   b. What you must do to be repaid.
7. Ask estimator to provide additional estimates:
   a. Guaranteed estimate—A binding estimate guaranteeing that you pay only the price quoted and no more. Ask for how long the price is guaranteed.
   b. Not-over estimate—An estimate guaranteed not to be over a specified amount in spite of the actual shipment weight. If weight on which estimate is based is *greater* than the estimate, you pay only the estimated amount. If

weight is *less* than the estimate, you pay an amount based on the actual shipment weight.

   c. Discounted estimate—An estimate for which some or all services are discounted from rates stated in published tariff books. If published rates increase between your estimate and your move, your cost often increases, even if you receive the same discount. Consider:

- Requesting to see the rates stated in the tariff book.
- Asking how much the rates you were quoted are discounted.
- Inquiring for how long this discount applies.
- Asking when the estimator expects the next rate increase.

8. If your estimate is the guaranteed or not-over type, ask when you move whether you qualify to have extra items added without paying any additional fees. (Due to the manner in which tariff books are set up combined with the estimated weight of your goods, your shipment may or may not qualify.)

9. Make sure that each estimate is complete and accurate. Estimates are good *only* for items listed in estimate.

10. Tell each estimator that you will not be making a decision at this time because you want to compare estimates.

11. Compare estimates and choose the company that you want to move your goods.

12. Call the company you have chosen and ask the customer service person to prepare an order for service. Consider being sure that the order is:

- A complete and accurate list of items you want to move.
  - You can add or delete items after you sign the service order and before you move by signing an addendum stating what you are adding or deleting.
  - Companies usually charge extra for added items.
  - Drivers may refuse to load unlisted items.
- Cancelable by you at any time without a charge because the service order is *not* a contract.

13. Driver will ask you to sign a bill of lading, which is the contract between you and the moving company. Sign the bill of lading only when you are sure that the bill:

- Is correct.
- Corresponds in all details to the estimate, the service order, *and* the addenda.
- States the following:
  - The company's responsibilities and liability.
  - Your responsibilities.
  - The services to be rendered and their prices.

14. When the van arrives to load or unload your shipment:

a. Accompany the person who is doing the inventory.

b. Be sure all items are listed and their condition are accurately described on your and their inventory sheets.

c. If you do not agree with the person's description of condition, note your description and initial the note on both sheets.

d. Sign sheets *only* when you feel everything is listed and accurately described.

15. File a claim after the move for lost items, damaged items, and/or extra expenses incurred if delivery was delayed through no fault of yours.

ADVANTAGES

- Everything can be moved at one time.
- Movers are trained to move your goods quickly and effectively.
- This method is less tiring and involves less chance of injury for you.
- Movers must estimate costs correctly within certain limits.

DISADVANTAGES

- This method is expensive.
- You must pay when you are moved because most moving companies do not accept credit cards.

Move It Yourself

Moving your goods yourself is based on size and type of vehicle, accessories, type of move, and insurance.

Cost Factors

The cost of moving is based on several factors.

Size of Vehicle. To determine the size of vehicle you need for the move, consider:

1. Getting estimates from professional movers for several items including:
   a. The full move.
   b. Moving selected items. Get a breakdown of costs so if you decide to do various aspects yourself you can judge how much you might save.
   c. The number of cubic feet of area the load will occupy. Remember, chances are that you are not as adept at loading and may use more space than a professional.

2. Obtaining information from vehicle rental companies and following their instructions for estimating. They may:
   a. Suggest you do an inventory and add the estimated cubic feet that each item you move occupies.
   b. Recommend a vehicle to use by the size of your home.

Type of Vehicle. The vehicle you rent may depend on the type of move you make.

- Local moves give you more options; you may:
  - Rent a large vehicle and move everything at once.
  - Rent a smaller vehicle and move over a longer period of time. This enables you to use some items such as pads, straps, and perhaps even some cartons several times. It also permits you to rest between loads and not drive yourself to exhaustion.
- Long-distance moves are generally most effectively handled using the largest vehicle that accommodates your belongings and that you can handle comfortably and safely.

Moving Accessories. In addition to the truck, consider renting the following:

- Hand truck or dolly—A heavy-duty hand truck with straps is designed for moving large, heavy items like appliances but is useful even for stacks of boxes.
- Furniture blankets/pads and straps—Strap blankets or pads on furniture for protection.
- Extension mirrors—For safety, consider using extension mirrors on *both* sides, whether you are renting a vehicle that lacks extension mirrors or are using your own vehicle to tow a trailer.

Insurance. Movers usually include coverage against damage and loss based on required minimum amount per pound *if* you request coverage. The actual value of items is usually much greater than the minimum per-pound coverage. The actual value is the depreciated value of the item at the present time, not the full cost of replacing the item. Consider:

- Obtaining higher coverage than the minimum provided at least to the actual value if not to the replacement value.
- Inquiring about what options for liability coverage are available through the moving company and their costs.
- Obtaining temporary coverage for the move if your homeowner's policy does not contain moving coverage.

Type of Move. The move you make also determines the amount the rental company charges.

- For round trips, you rent the vehicle and return it to the same dealer. For trailers, you generally pay a daily charge; for trucks, you usually pay a daily rate plus mileage. Be sure you have a binding reservation for a round-trip rental; otherwise, you may not find a vehicle available even though you have reserved one. Dealers prefer to rent to one-way movers because income is greater for the amount of work involved.

- For one-way trips, you rent a vehicle from one dealer and return it to another dealer.
  ○ Ask a renting dealer to look for a drop-off point that is handy to your destination and has the lowest charges.
  ○ Reserve your vehicle well in advance, particularly if you desire automatic transmission, air conditioning, and/or a loading ramp or hydraulic lift gate.

Travel Expenses. You will have some travel expenses no matter how you travel to your new home. If you move your own goods, some of these expenses will be greater than usual.

- Gas consumption approximations can be obtained from the dealer from whom you rent the vehicle.
- Road taxes, charged by some states that require trip permits, and tolls are often higher with a truck or trailer. An automobile club may have information about these costs.
- Lodging and food costs increase if you travel more slowly.

Deposits. Deposits are up-front costs on the equipment you rent, which the rental company refunds after you return the equipment. The company may deduct charges from the deposit, including extra mileage or time, loss of or damage to equipment, and gas (if you return the vehicle filled with less gas than when you received it).

ADVANTAGES
- This method is less expensive than using professionals.
- Agencies usually accept credit cards; you can pay later.
- You can move at a convenient time.

DISADVANTAGES
- You may break or mar some of the items you move.
- You may become physically and emotionally exhausted.
- You may hurt yourself packing and lifting heavy objects.
- You may be liable if someone is hurt while helping you.
- You may be more apt to have a traffic accident while using equipment to which you are not accustomed.
- You may estimate expenses incorrectly.

Other Savings

Save money when you move by:

1. Sending out items for cleaning or repair *before* moving, then have items delivered or pick them up after you move (for local moves).
2. Obtaining cartons that fit your needs.
   a. Obtaining cartons at local stores. Ask employees of liquor stores, supermarkets, and office supplies and computer

stores to save sturdy cartons with tops for you. Also try moving companies with supplies of boxes from unpacking other people's moves.

b. Buying cartons from moving companies, both commercial and do-it-yourself that may:
   - Sell book, dish, and wardrobe cartons, in addition to utility cartons in several sizes. Because they are uniform, these cartons are more easily loaded than an assortment from various sources.
   - Have cartons constructed to meet the needs of the loads they are designed to carry.
   - Offer recommendations about what to pack in which size cartons and how to pack.

c. Packing some items yourself, at least clothes and unbreakables.

d. Shipping heavy items you will not need immediately by slower, less expensive methods.
   - Consider shipping items such as books, magazines, some appliances, piano or organ, pool table, sports equipment, and vehicles.
   - For rates, contact carriers including cartage, express, and freight-forwarding companies and parcel-shipping services, including the post office, bus companies, and railroads.

3. Using a combination of methods:
   a. Have movers pack and move heavy items that you need right away or find hard to handle.
   b. Pack and ship heavy items you do not need immediately by slower, less expensive methods.
   c. Pack and move lightweight items yourself.
   d. Keep valuables with you.

Step 3: Inventory Your Home

An inventory can take the form of a written list, photos, videos, and/or receipts. In case of items lost or damaged during your move, burglary, or disasters (such as fire or flood), you will have information for insurance purposes. For the most complete inventory, use a combination of these methods of recording your home's contents.

Written List

List items by name, how many you have, the year they were purchased, and their present value. This method is inexpensive but time-consuming to use. Combined with photographs or videos, it provides good coverage.

Receipts

Keep the original receipt or a copy for each major item you have on your inventory. Store the receipts in a lockbox or other safe place outside your home in case of fire or other disaster. This method is easy and provides the best documentation. It provides the best protection when combined with photographs or videos.

Photographs or Videos

Take photographs or videos of the items as they are placed in your home. Take closeups of especially valuable items. This method may be relatively expensive, especially if you must rent equipment and buy the film or tapes. It provides proof of the condition of the items.

Step 4: Handle Address Changes and Records Transfers

Use the Address Change & Records Transfer Worksheet in Section VI, "Worksheets and Contracts," to aid you in notifying your correspondents of your address change and transferring your records.

Prepare Address Change & Records Transfer Worksheet

Address Changes

To handle your change of address, record the names and addresses of the professionals and companies on the form, noting especially those from which you need to transfer records.

1. Make an *X* in the Address column and write data requested about parties to whom you want to send address change notices.
2. Prepare address change notices.
   a. Get postcard address-change forms at your local post office or use your own postcards or letters.
   b. Include the date that the address change takes effect.
3. Make an *X* in the Did column as you prepare each notice.
4. Mail the notices.

Records Transfer

1. Make an *X* in the Record column and write information about the party *from* whom you wish records to be transferred.
2. On the next line write *To* in Record column and write data about party *to* whom you wish records transferred.
3. Contact the parties from whom you wish the records to be transferred. Inform them that:

a. You want records transferred.

b. The name and address to whom you wish the records to be sent.

4. When you have sent a letter or contacted the party by telephone, make an *X* in the Did column.

Step 5: Stop (and Possibly Start) Services

To stop services at your old home and start them at your new home, complete and use the Stop & Start Services Worksheet in Section VI, "Worksheets and Contracts."

Thank you for using this book to successfully sell your home yourself. After you have settled in your new location, we would like to hear from you, in care of the publisher, about your experience using *How to Sell Your Home Without a Broker, Third Edition.* Thank you, again! God bless!

SECTION VI
Worksheets and Contracts

Worksheets

Contracts

ACCOUNTANT QUESTIONS WORKSHEET

Accountant:_____   Telephone:_____

Address:_____

Ask	Question	Answer
	What are your credentials?	
	What do you charge per hour?	$ /hour
	Will you provide a list of items currently considered capital improvements?	☐ Yes ☐ No
	What is my tax result leasing to buyers before closing?	$
	What is my tax result leasing from buyers after closing?	$
	What is my tax result using a lease option?	$
	Names & phone numbers of attorneys you recommend?	
	Names & phone numbers of closing agents you recommend?	
	Names & phone numbers of escrow holders you recommend?	
	Names & phone numbers of real estate professionals you recommend?	
	Names & phone numbers of title companies you recommend?	
	If I carry back a loan, what are my tax consequences?	
	If I use an AITD or wraparound loan, what tax rules apply?	
	What moving costs are currently tax deductible?	
	What expenses of the sale are currently tax deductible?	
	What is the effect of installment sale imputed tax rate?	
	What is the effect of conversion of my residence to a rental?	
	What is the effect of FIRPTA regulations on my transaction?	
	How much do I owe in taxes on my home sale?	

ADDRESS CHANGE & RECORDS TRANSFER WORKSHEET

Name: _____

Old Address: _____

New Address: _____

Date: _____

Add.	Rec.	Name	Address	Telephone	Did
Type:					
Type:					
Type:					
Type:					

ADDRESS CHANGE & RECORDS TRANSFER WORKSHEET

Use Address Change & Records Transfer Worksheet as follows: List to the right of the word *Type* the type of people or organizations to whom you would like to send your address change or from whom you would like to have records transferred. Suggested people or organizations include the following:

* Accountants and Tax Preparers
* Attorneys
* Banks, Savings & Loans, etc.
* Catalog Companies
* Credit & Debit Card Companies
* Department Stores
* Friends and Relatives
* Governmental Agencies (motor vehicle departments, post office, Social Security Administration, Veterans' Administration, voter registration, etc.)
* Insurance Agents and Companies

* Investments (bonds, certificates of deposit, stocks, stockbrokers, etc.)
* Lenders and Borrowers (mortgages, personal loans, trust deeds)
* Magazines and Newspapers
* Medical (chiropractors, dentists, ophthamologists, pharmacies, physicians, veterinarians, etc.)
* Professional Organizations and Unions
* Religious Organizations
* Schools
* Tenants

ADVERTISING BUDGET WORKSHEET

Name:_____   Date:_____

Address:_____

Advertisement Type	Publication	#	Price Each	Subtotal
Signs				
For Sale by Owner				
Open House				
Flags				
Banners				
Newspaper Ads				
Classified				
Advertisement #1				
Advertisement #2				
Display				
Advertisement #1				
Advertisement #2				
Newsletter Ads				
Advertisement #1				
Advertisement #2				
Magazine Ads				
Advertisement #1				
Advertisement #2				
Flyers				
Pictures				
Paper				
Printing				
Distribution				
Open Houses				
Announcements				
Refreshments				
Internet Ads				
			TOTAL	

ANSWERING MACHINE OR VOICE MAIL MESSAGE

Name:_____ Telephone:_____

Address_____

Record This Message

Thank you for calling.

You have reached _____ (your telephone number). Our home is for sale.

Our home is in the _____ section of _____ (city).

The property has ____ bedrooms, _____ baths, and approximately _____ square feet of living space.

This property also has the following (list important features):

_____,

_____,

_____,

_____, and

_____.

The price of our home is $_____.

If you would like to see the property, at the sound of the tone please leave your name and number, as well as any questions you may have. We will return your call as soon as possible. Thank you.

ASKING PRICE DETERMINATION WORKSHEET

Name: _____

Address: _____

Date: _____

PROPERTY INFORMATION						PRICE	
Property Address	BRs	BAs	Square Feet	Remarks		For Sale	Sold
Source:			☐ Appraiser	☐ Neighbors	☐ Real Estate Professional	☐ Title Company	
Source:			☐ Appraiser	☐ Neighbors	☐ Real Estate Professional	☐ Title Company	
Source:			☐ Appraiser	☐ Neighbors	☐ Real Estate Professional	☐ Title Company	
MY HOME							
MOST COMPARABLES					For Sale		
					Sold		
						ASKING PRICE	

ATTORNEY QUESTIONS WORKSHEET

Attorney:_____ Telephone:_____
Address:_____

Ask	Question	Answer
	What are your credentials?	
	Do you specialize in real estate?	☐ Yes ☐ No
	What do you charge per hour?	$ /hour
	Will you represent me?	☐ Yes ☐ No
	How much deposit do you suggest I ask for?	$
	Does my loan have a prepayment penalty?	☐ Yes ☐ No
	If yes, how much prepayment penalty can be charged?	$
	Is my loan assumable?	☐ Yes ☐ No
	If yes, can the lender charge an assumption fee?	☐ Yes ☐ No
	If yes, how much assumption fee can be charged?	$
	Does lender require buyer qualification to assume loan?	☐ Yes ☐ No
	Does lender require loan renegotiation to assume loan?	☐ Yes ☐ No
	Is my loan a "subject-to" loan?	☐ Yes ☐ No
	Is my loan due on sale?	☐ Yes ☐ No
	Do you recommend I use a seller buy-down loan?	☐ Yes ☐ No
	If yes, for how much?	$
	If yes, for how long?	
	Do you recommend I use a seller carry-back loan?	☐ Yes ☐ No
	If yes, for how much?	$
	If yes, for how long?	
	If yes, will you qualify the buyers?	☐ Yes ☐ No
	If yes, will you write the loan agreement?	☐ Yes ☐ No
	Do you recommend I use an AITD or wraparound mortgage?	☐ Yes ☐ No
	If yes, for how much?	$
	If yes, for how long?	
	If yes, will you qualify the buyers?	☐ Yes ☐ No
	If yes, will you write the contract?	☐ Yes ☐ No
	Do you suggest I use a lease?	☐ Yes ☐ No
	If yes, for how much?	$
	If yes, for how long?	
	Do you suggest I use a lease option?	☐ Yes ☐ No
	If yes, for how much?	$
	If yes, for how long?	
	If yes, will you write the lease option?	☐ Yes ☐ No
	Names & phone numbers of accountants you recommend?	
	Names & phone numbers of appraisers you recommend?	
	Names & phone numbers of closing agents you recommend?	

(continued)

ATTORNEY QUESTIONS WORKSHEET

Attorney:_____ Telephone:_____

Address:_____

Ask	Question	Answer
	Names & phone numbers of escrow holders you recommend?	
	Names & phone numbers of home inspectors you recommend?	
	Names & phone numbers of pest control operators you recommend?	
	Names & phone numbers of real estate professionals you recommend?	
	Names & phone numbers of title companies you recommend?	
	Are you a closing agent/escrow holder?	☐ Yes ☐ No
	If yes, how many closings/escrows do you handle per year?	
	If yes, will you handle my closing/escrow?	☐ Yes ☐ No
	Will you review my contracts for improvements?	☐ Yes ☐ No
	What are the mechanic's lien laws that apply to this contract?	
	What sign laws should I be aware of in this community?	
	What laws regarding discrimination apply to this sale?	
	What laws regarding real estate disclosure apply to this sale?	
	Is a physical inspection necessary by law?	☐ Yes ☐ No
	If yes, who must pay?	
	If no, do you suggest I have a physical inspection?	☐ Yes ☐ No
	Is a geological inspection necessary by law?	☐ Yes ☐ No
	If yes, who must pay?	
	If no, do you suggest I have a geological inspection?	☐ Yes ☐ No
	Is a pest control inspection necessary by law?	☐ Yes ☐ No
	How much initial deposit do you suggest?	$
	By how much do you suggest buyers increase the deposit?	$
	How much down payment do you recommend?	$
	Do you suggest buyers get a new loan?	☐ Yes ☐ No
	Do you suggest buyers assume my loan?	☐ Yes ☐ No
	Do you suggest buyers take title "subject to"?	☐ Yes ☐ No
	Do you suggest I make a seller carry-back loan?	☐ Yes ☐ No
	If yes, for how much?	$
	If yes, for how long?	
	Do you suggest leasing to buyers before closing?	☐ Yes ☐ No
	If yes, for how much?	$
	Do you suggest leasing from buyers after closing?	☐ Yes ☐ No
	If yes, for how much?	$
	Do you suggest I use a lease option?	☐ Yes ☐ No
	If yes, for how much?	$
	If yes, for how long?	

(continued)

ATTORNEY QUESTIONS WORKSHEET

Attorney:_____ Telephone:_____

Address:_____

Ask	Question	Answer
	Do you suggest I use a purchase option?	☐ Yes ☐ No
	If yes, for how much?	$
	If yes, for how long?	
	Do you suggest I use an escrow?	☐ Yes ☐ No
	If yes, for how long?	
	If yes, by whom do you suggest escrow fees be paid?	
	What type of title insurance do you recommend?	
	By whom do you recommend the title insurance fees be paid?	
	As of what date do you suggest prorations be calculated?	
	Who pays the transfer tax on this transaction?	
	What date do you suggest buyers take possession?	
	What regulations apply regarding smoke detectors?	
	Is Flood Hazard Area Disclosure required?	☐ Yes ☐ No
	Is disclosure for earthquake potential required?	☐ Yes ☐ No
	Do you suggest I renegotiate with this buyer?	☐ Yes ☐ No
	Do you suggest I remarket my home?	☐ Yes ☐ No

ATTRACTIVENESS WORKSHEET

Name:_____   Date:_____

Address:_____

Do	By	Date	Job Description	Contractor & phone number *or* Material needed	Cost Estimate	Did
\multicolumn{7}{c}{Jobs to Be Done}
			Lawn and Plantings			
			Lawn mowed and edged			
			Lawn raked			
			Shrubs trimmed			
			Plantings watered			
			Toys picked up			
			Pet messes removed			
			Hoses rolled			
			Other:			
			Driveways and Walks			
			Swept			
			Orderly			
			Other:			
			Patios, Decks, Courts			
			Swept			
			Orderly			
			Other:			
			Pools and Spas			
			Vacuumed			
			Chlorinated			
			Other:			
			Entrance			
			Clutter free			
			Lights clean			
			Walls clean			
			Windows & sills clean			
			Doors & woodwork clean			
			Hardware polished			
			Floors & mats clean			
			Other:			
				Subtotal #1		

(continued)

ATTRACTIVENESS WORKSHEET

Name:_____   Date:_____

Address:_____

Jobs to Be Done						
Do	By	Date	**Job Description**	**Contractor & phone number** *or* **Material needed**	**Cost Estimate**	Did
			Room:			
			Clutter free			
			Lights clean			
			Walls clean			
			Windows & sills clean			
			Doors & woodwork clean			
			Fireplace clean			
			Carpet/floors clean			
			Furniture clean			
			Furniture arranged			
			Other:			
			Bedroom #:			
			Clutter free			
			Lights clean			
			Walls clean			
			Windows & sills clean			
			Doors & woodwork clean			
			Carpet/floors clean			
			Furniture clean			
			Furniture arranged			
			Other:			
			Bathroom #:			
			Clutter free			
			Lights clean			
			Walls & trim clean			
			Windows & sills clean			
			Doors & woodwork clean			
			Sink, tub, & toilet clean			
			Grout lines clean			
			Hardware polished			
			Carpet/floors clean			
			Other:			
				Subtotal #		

(continued)

ATTRACTIVENESS WORKSHEET

Name:_____ Date:_____

Address:_____

Jobs to Be Done						
Do	By	Date	Job Description	Contractor & phone number *or* Material needed	Cost Estimate	Did
			Kitchen			
			Clutter free			
			Lights clean			
			Walls clean			
			Windows & sills clean			
			Doors & woodwork clean			
			Sink & disposal clean			
			Ovens & stoves clean			
			Cupboards orderly			
			Carpet/floors clean			
			Other:			
			Hall and Stairs			
			Clutter free			
			Lights clean			
			Walls clean			
			Windows & sills clean			
			Doors & woodwork clean			
			Carpet/floors clean			
			Furniture clean			
			Furniture arranged			
			Other:			
			Garage or Carport			
			Clutter free			
			Lights clean			
			Windows & sills clean			
			Floors clean			
			Other:			
				Subtotal #		

Subtotal # 1	
Subtotal #	
Subtotal #	
Subtotal #	
Subtotal #	
TOTAL	

CAPITAL IMPROVEMENTS WORKSHEET

Name:_____ Date:_____

Address:_____

Did	Improvement	Date	Cost
	Yard		
	Yard area enlarged		
	Shrubs added		
	Trees added		
	Sprinkler system added		
	Decorative component redesigned		
	Decorative component added		
	Resurfacing for drainage		
	Equipment installed for drainage		
	Other:		
	Driveways, Walks, Walls, and Fences		
	Driveway added or extended		
	Walk added or extended		
	Curb addition or extension		
	Walls and/or fences added or extended		
	Other:		
	Patios, Decks, and Courts		
	Patio enlarged or added		
	Deck enlarged or added		
	Game court (e.g., tennis) added		
	Other:		
	Pools and Spas		
	Pool installed		
	Spa installed		
	Sauna installed		
	Changing facilities installed		
	Other:		
	Structures		
	Toolshed improved or added		
	Greenhouse improved or added		
	Outbuilding improved or added		
	Barn improved or added		
	Stable improved or added		
	Other:		
	Subtotal #1		

(continued)

CAPITAL IMPROVEMENTS WORKSHEET

Name:_____ Date:_____

Address:_____

Did	Improvement	Date	Cost
	Outdoor Equipment		
	Lighting equipment installed		
	Sound system installed		
	Barbecue installed		
	Playground equipment installed		
	Well installed		
	Pump installed		
	Incinerator installed		
	Other:		
	Roofs and Gutters		
	Roof upgrades		
	Gutter upgrades		
	Other:		
	Siding, Walls, and Foundation		
	Siding upgrades		
	Wall upgrades		
	Structural strengthening		
	Foundation work for settling and seepage		
	Floor jack installed		
	Other:		
	Windows and Doors		
	Windows and screens installed		
	Shutters installed		
	Awning upgraded or installed		
	Door installed		
	Storm door installed		
	Other:		
	Entrance		
	Intercom installed		
	Security system installed		
	Ceiling or walls upgraded		
	Lighting fixtures upgraded or installed		
	Floor covering permanently installed		
	Other:		
	Subtotal #2		

(continued)

CAPITAL IMPROVEMENTS WORKSHEET

Name:_____ Date:_____

Address:_____

Did	Improvement	Date	Cost
	Kitchen		
	Ceiling upgraded		
	Light fixture(s) upgraded or installed		
	Floor covering permanently installed		
	Furnishings built in/counter(s) added		
	Closets, cabinets, or shelves added		
	Ovens/stoves built in		
	Sink(s) added		
	Garbage disposal added		
	Dishwasher added		
	Refrigerator built in		
	Freezer built-in		
	Trash compactor added		
	Walls upgraded		
	Other:		
	Utilities		
	Electric system upgraded		
	Power lines upgraded or added		
	Plumbing upgraded or added		
	Heating system upgraded or added		
	Air-conditioning system upgraded or added		
	Humidifying/dehumidifying system upgraded or added		
	Air filtration system upgraded or added		
	Smoke/radon detectors upgraded or added		
	Water softener upgraded or added		
	Septic tank upgraded or added		
	Leach line upgraded or added		
	Other:		
	Garage/Carport		
	Ceiling upgraded		
	Light fixture(s) upgraded or installed		
	Floor covering permanently installed		
	Closets, cabinets, and/or shelves added		
	Plumbing fixtures added		
	Walls upgraded		
	Other:		
	Subtotal #3		

(continued)

CAPITAL IMPROVEMENTS WORKSHEET

Name:_____ Date:_____

Address:_____

Did	Improvement	Date	Cost
	Room:		
	Ceiling upgraded		
	Light fixture(s) upgraded or installed		
	Floor covering permanently installed		
	Furnishings built in		
	Closets, cabinets, or shelves added		
	Fireplace added		
	Entertainment equipment built in		
	Walls upgraded		
	Other:		
	Bedroom #:		
	Ceiling upgraded		
	Light fixture(s) upgraded or installed		
	Floor covering permanently installed		
	Furnishings built in		
	Closets, cabinets, or shelves added		
	Fireplace added		
	Walls upgraded		
	Other:		
	Bathroom #:		
	Ceiling upgraded		
	Light fixture(s) upgraded or installed		
	Floor covering permanently installed		
	Furnishings built in		
	Closets, cabinets, or shelves added		
	Plumbing fixtures upgraded or added		
	Walls upgraded		
	Other:		
	Subtotal #		

Subtotal # 1	
Subtotal # 2	
Subtotal # 3	
Subtotal #	
Subtotal #	
Subtotal #	
Subtotal #	
TOTAL	**$**

CLOSING AGENT/ESCROW QUESTIONS WORKSHEET

Agent/escrow:_____   Telephone:_____

Address:_____

Ask	Question	Answer
	What are your credentials?	
	How many transactions do you handle per year?	
	What do you charge?	$
	Do you mind answering my questions?	☐ Yes ☐ No
	Names & phone numbers of accountants you recommend?	
	Names & phone numbers of appraisers you recommend?	
	Names & phone numbers of home inspectors you recommend?	
	Names & phone numbers of lenders you recommend?	
	Names & phone numbers of title companies you recommend?	
	Names & phone numbers of real estate professionals you recommend?	
	Names & phone numbers of pest control operators you recommend?	
	What laws regarding discrimination apply to this sale?	
	What laws regarding transfer disclosure apply to this sale?	
	Is Flood Hazard Area Disclosure required?	☐ Yes ☐ No
	Is disclosure for earthquake potential required?	☐ Yes ☐ No
	Is a physical inspection necessary by law?	☐ Yes ☐ No
	If yes, who must pay?	
	Is a geological inspection necessary by law?	☐ Yes ☐ No
	If yes, who must pay?	
	Is a pest control inspection necessary by law?	☐ Yes ☐ No
	If yes, who must pay?	
	Your cost estimate for an appraisal fee?	$
	Your cost estimate for an assumption fee?	$
	Your cost estimate for beneficiary statement?	$
	Your cost estimate for closing/escrow fees?	$
	Who usually pays closing/escrow fees?	$
	Your cost estimate for credit report fee?	$
	Your cost estimate for delinquent payments on my account?	$
	Your cost estimate for demand fee?	$
	Your cost estimate for document preparation fees?	$
	Your cost estimate for drawing deed fees?	$
	Your cost estimate for hazard insurance costs?	$
	Your cost estimate for home warranty costs?	$
	Your cost estimate for impounds?	$
	Your cost estimate for interest?	$
	Your cost estimate for a loan tie-in fee?	$

(continued)

CLOSING AGENT/ESCROW QUESTIONS WORKSHEET

Agent/escrow:_____   Telephone:_____

Address:_____

Ask	Question	Answer
	Your cost estimate for a loan origination fee?	$
	Your cost estimate for notary fees?	$
	Your cost estimate for a pest control inspection fee?	$
	Who usually pays pest control inspection fees?	
	Your cost estimate for a physical inspection fee?	$
	Who usually pays physical inspection fees?	
	Your cost estimate for points?	$
	Your cost estimate for a prepayment penalty?	$
	Your cost estimate for a reconveyance deed?	$
	Your cost estimate for a recording fee?	$
	Your cost estimate for satisfaction of mortgage?	$
	Your cost estimate for the title insurance?	$
	Your cost estimate for the transfer fee?	$
	Your cost estimate for transfer tax?	$
	How do I calculate the transfer tax?	
	As of what date do you suggest prorations be calculated?	
	What regulations apply regarding smoke detectors?	
	How do I set up a closing or escrow?	
	What information do you need for closing or setting up an escrow?	
	What responsibilities do I have for escrow?	
	What is your procedure for amending escrow instructions?	
	Do you require a walk-through inspection before closing?	☐ Yes ☐ No
	If yes, what timing do you suggest on the walk-through?	
	What else needs to be done so that closing can occur?	
	When do you think closing will occur?	

CONDITIONS WORKSHEET

☐ WORKING   ☐ COUNTEROFFER

Address: _____

Seller: _____ Buyer: _____

Date prepared: _____ Closing date: _____

For complete wording of each section, see your (the seller's) copy of the purchase contract.

Used	Met	Condition
		Additional Financing Terms (see Loans, Additonal Terms)
		Additional Terms and Conditions (see the specific term or condition)
		Balance of Down Payment (see Down Payment, Balance)
		Buyer Approval
		Written notification of disapproval
		Within _____ days
		Balances adjusted in: ☐ cash ☐ other:
		Closing (see Escrow)
		Condition of Property
		Condominium/PUD
		Buyers allowed _____ days from receipt to review documents
		Buyers approve
		Buyers fail to notify seller in writing of disapproval (considered approval)
		Deposit (see Down Payment, Deposit)
		Diligence and Good Faith to Obtain Financing
		Down Payment, Deposit
		Deposited into:
		Amount: $
		Down Payment, Increased Deposit
		Within _____ days
		Deposited into:
		Amount: $
		Down Payment, Balance
		Deposited into:
		On or before:
		Amount: $

(continued)

CONDITIONS WORKSHEET

☐ WORKING   ☐ COUNTEROFFER

Address:_____

Seller:_____   Buyer:_____

Date prepared:_____   Closing date:_____

For complete wording of each section, see your (the seller's) copy of the purchase contract.

Used	Met	Condition
		Energy Conservation Retrofit
		☐ Buyer ☐ Seller to comply with
		☐ Buyer ☐ Seller to pay for
		Escrow
		Signed instructions to:
		Within _____ days from seller's acceptance
		Closing within _____ days from seller's acceptance
		Existing First Loan (see Loan, First Existing)
		Existing Second Loan (see Loan, Second Existing)
		Geological Inspection
		Buyers select professional within _____ days after seller's acceptance
		Buyers deliver to seller within _____ days after seller's acceptance written claims of defects and written reports
		Buyers approved
		Buyers fail to give seller written notice of disapproval (considered approval)
		Home Protection Plan (Home Warranty)
		To be issued by:
		Cost not to exceed: $
		Increased Deposit (See Down Payment, Increased Deposit)
		Loan, First Existing
		Buyers to: ☐ Assume ☐ Take title subject to
		Approximate balance of: $
		In favor of:
		Payable monthly at: $
		Interest at: %
		Loan: ☐ Fixed rate ☐ Other:
		Fees not to exceed: $

(continued)

CONDITIONS WORKSHEET

☐ WORKING   ☐ COUNTEROFFER

Address:_____

Seller:_____ Buyer:_____

Date prepared:_____ Closing date:_____

For complete wording of each section, see your (the seller's) copy of the purchase contract.

Used	Met	Condition
		Loan, First New
		Amount: $
		Payable: ☐ Biweekly ☐ Monthly
		At approximately: $
		Interest at origination not to exceed: %
		Loan: ☐ Fixed rate ☐ Other:
		All due in _____ years
		Loan fee not to exceed : $
		Maximum of _____ FHA/VA discount points
		Loan, Second Existing
		Assume
		Take title subject to
		Balance of: $
		In favor of:
		Payable monthly at: $
		Interest at: %
		Loan: ☐ Fixed rate ☐ Other:
		Buyers' fees not to exceed : $
		Loan, Second New
		Amount: $
		Payable: ☐ Biweekly ☐ Monthly
		At approximately: $
		Interest at origination: %
		Loan: ☐ Fixed rate ☐ Other:
		All due in _____ years
		Buyers' fees not to exceed: $

(continued)

CONDITIONS WORKSHEET

☐ WORKING   ☐ COUNTEROFFER

Address:_____

Seller:_____   Buyer:_____

Date prepared:_____   Closing date:_____

For complete wording of each section, see your (the seller's) copy of the purchase contract.

Used	Met	Condition
		Loan Secured by Deed of Trust in Favor of Seller
		Deed of trust ☐ 1st ☐ 2nd ☐ 3rd
		Amount: $
		Payable monthly at: $
		Interest at: %
		All due: ☐ _____ years ☐ upon sale ☐ upon transfer
		Late charge of: $
		Within _____ days of due date
		Loan, Additional Terms
		Note Secured by Deed of Trust in Favor of Seller (see Loan Secured by Deed of Trust in Favor of Seller)
		Other Terms and Conditions

(continued)

CONDITIONS WORKSHEET

☐ WORKING   ☐ COUNTEROFFER

Address: _____

Seller: _____   Buyer: _____

Date prepared: _____   Closing date: _____

For complete wording of each section, see your (the seller's) copy of the purchase contract.

Used	Met	Condition
		Pest Control
		Within _____ days of seller's acceptance
		Written inspection report by:
		Inspection of inaccessible areas
		Work to repair damage
		Work to correct conditions that cause infestation
		Work to correct conditions that are likely to cause infestation
		Other:
		Physical Inspection
		Buyers to select inspector within _____ days
		Written claims of defects delivered to seller within _____ days
		Planned Unit Development (see Condominium/PUD)
		Possession
		Possession delivered to buyers on close of escrow (COE)
		Possession delivered to buyers not later than _____ days after COE
		Other:
		Price, Total Purchase $
		Smoke Detector(s)
		State requirements met
		Local requirements met
		Written statement of compliance
		Special Studies Zone Disclosure
		Within _____ days from date of seller's acceptance
		Buyers approved
		Buyers failed to notify seller in writing of disapproval (considered approval)

(continued)

CONDITIONS WORKSHEET

☐ WORKING   ☐ COUNTEROFFER

Address: _____

Seller: _____   Buyer: _____

Date prepared: _____   Closing date: _____

For complete wording of each section, see your (the seller's) copy of the purchase contract.

Used	Met	Condition
		Supplements
		Interim Occupancy Agreement
		Residential Lease Agreement after Sale
		VA and FHA Amendments
		Tax Withholding
		Seller provides buyers an affidavit
		Seller provides buyers a qualifying statement
		Title
		Not disapproved by buyers in writing
		Within _____ days of receipt of current preliminary report
		Seller furnishes buyers with a standard title insurance policy
		Seller furnishes buyers with an extended title insurance policy
		Policy issued by:
		Seller is willing and able to eliminate buyers' disapprovals
		Total Purchase Price (see Price, Total Purchase)
		Transfer Disclosure
		Buyer has received and read
		Seller provides buyers with real estate disclosure within _____ days

ESTIMATE OF PROCEEDS WORKSHEET

☐ **PRELIMINARY**   ☐ **WORKING**   ☐ **COUNTEROFFER**

Seller:_____   Buyer:_____

Address:_____

Selling price:_____   Financing type:_____

Date prepared:_____   Proposed closing date:_____

COSTS ESTIMATE			
Pay	Cost	Amount	Notes
	Appraisal fee		
	Assessments		
	Assumption fee		
	Attorney fees		
	Beneficiary statement		
	Credit report		
	Delinquent payments		
	Demand fees		
	Document preparation		
	Drawing deed		
	Escrow/closing fees		
	Homeowner's assn. fee		
	Homeowner's insurance		
	Home warranty		
	Impounds		
	Interest		
	Loan origination fee		
	Loan tie-in fee		
	Notary fee		
	Pest control inspection		
	Pest control repair		
	Physical inspection fee		
	Points		
	Prepayment penalty		
	Property taxes		
	Reconveyance fee		
	Recording fee		
	Satisfaction of mortgage		
	Subescrow fee		
	Survey fee		
	Title insurance		
	Title search fee		
	Transfer tax		
	Other:		
TOTAL COSTS ESTIMATE			

(continued)

ESTIMATE OF PROCEEDS WORKSHEET

☐ **PRELIMINARY**   ☐ **WORKING**   ☐ **COUNTEROFFER**

Seller:_____ Buyer:_____

Address:_____

Selling price:_____ Financing type:_____

Date prepared:_____ Proposed closing date:_____

PRORATION INSTRUCTIONS

1. Assume a 30-day month and a 360-day year for estimate purposes.
    (To borrow days from Month column, subtract 1 month from Month column and add 30 days to Day column. To borrow months from Year column, subtract 1 year from Year column and add 12 months to Month column.)
2. Seller does not pay costs for the day of closing.
3. For items for which you have **not paid**, such as interest and property taxes, enter value on the proper line under the heading Costs Estimate.
4. For items for which you **prepaid**, such as insurance, taxes, and rents, enter value on the proper line under the heading Credits Estimate.

CALCULATIONS

Total Days for Which Payment Applies

Calculation of Years, Months, & Days	Year	Month	Day		Conversion to Number of Days				
Ending					Years		X 360 =	+	days
- Starting					Months		X 30 =	+	days
= Total Years, Months, Days					Days		X 1 =	+	days
						Total Days		=	

Actual Days for Which Seller Must Pay

Calculation of Years, Months, & Days	Year	Month	Day		Conversion to Number of Days				
Ending					Years		X 360 =	+	days
- Starting					Months		X 30 =	+	days
= Total Years, Months, Days					Days		X 1 =	+	days
						Actual Days		=	

Payment Per Day

Total payment required	$
Total days	
Payment per	$

Seller's Payment Required

Payment per day	$
Actual days	
Seller's Payment	$

Seller's Credit for Item Paid in Advance

Payment per day	$
Actual days	
Seller's Credit for Item Paid In	$

(continued)

ESTIMATE OF PROCEEDS WORKSHEET

☐ **PRELIMINARY** ☐ **WORKING** ☐ **COUNTEROFFER**

Seller:_____ Buyer:_____

Address:_____

Selling price:_____ Financing type:_____

Date prepared:_____ Proposed closing date:_____

ENCUMBRANCES ESTIMATE

Pay	Encumbrance	Amount	Notes
	First loan		
	Second loan		
	Third loan		
	Improvement bonds		
	Liens		
	Other		
Total Encumbrances Estimate			

CREDITS ESTIMATE

Pay	Encumbrance	Amount	Notes
	Assessments		
	Bonds		
	Homeowner's assn. dues		
	Impounds		
	Insurance		
	Interest		
	Property taxes		
	Rental payments		
Total Credits Estimate	$		

DEBITS ESTIMATE

Total estimated costs	$	From page 1	
+ Total estimated encumbrances		From page 2	
Total Debits Estimate	$		

SELLER'S PROCEEDS ESTIMATE

Proposed selling price	$	From page 1	
- Total estimated debits		From page 2	
= Subtotal			
+ Total estimated credits			
Total Seller's Proceeds Estimate	$		

SELLER'S CASH FROM SALE ESTIMATE

Seller's proceeds estimate	$	
- Note financed by seller (you)		
Total Seller's Cash from Sale Estimate	$	

FINAL TAX IMPLICATIONS WORKSHEET

Name: _____ Date: _____

Address: _____

Gain on Sale of Old Residence	
1. Adjusted sales price of old residence	
Sales price of old residence	$
Closing costs of old residence	- $
Adjusted sales price of old	= $
2. Adjusted basis of old residence	
Basis of old residence from IRS Form 2119	$
Capital improvements on old residence from Capital Improvements	+ $
Worksheet	
Adjusted basis of old	= $
3. Gain on sale of old residence	
Adjusted **sales price** of old residence	$
Adjusted **basis** of old residence	- $
Gain on sale of old	= $
4. Taxable Gain (use one only)	
A. For married persons gain on sale of old residence	$
$500,000 exclusion	- $ 500,000.00
Taxable gain	= $
B. For single persons	
Gain on sale of old residence	$
$250,000 exclusion	- $ 250,000.00
Taxable gain	= $

FINISHING TOUCHES CHECKLIST

Name:_____

Address:_____

1. Make copies of this checklist.
2. Use a fresh checklist every time you handle the finishing touches to show your home.

Date:

Do	Did	Action	Notes
		Dressed to look successful	
		Property orderly	
		Walking made safe	
		Pets secured	
		Quiet or pleasing sounds created	
		Air temperature pleasant	
		Lights on	
		Window coverings open	
		Benefits displayed	
		Pleasing visual images set out	
		Pleasing smells	
		Bathrooms checked	

Date:

Do	Did	Action	Notes
		Dressed to look successful	
		Property orderly	
		Walking made safe	
		Pets secured	
		Quiet or pleasing sounds created	
		Air temperature pleasant	
		Lights on	
		Window coverings open	
		Benefits displayed	
		Pleasing visual images set out	
		Pleasing smells	
		Bathrooms checked	

GOALS/NEGOTIATING GOALS WORKSHEET

Name:_____　Date:_____

Address:_____

#	☐ GOALS:	☐ Preliminary	☐ Prioritized
	☐ NEGOTIATING GOALS	☐ Preliminary	☐ Prioritized

GUEST REGISTER

Name: _____

Address: _____

Date: _____

Date	Name	Address	Telephone Number

HOME FOR SALE FLYER

Put a photograph   or maybe two
in this area   before copying

General Information		Price: $		
Community:		Mortgage/TD	1st	2nd
Approximate Size: square feet		Payment:		
Cross Streets:		Lender:		
Telephone:		Due date:		
Style:		Take over:		
Exterior:		Interest %		
Roof type: Roof age:		**School Information**		
Home Age: # of stories:		Elementary:		
Lot size: Approx. _____ x _____ feet		Junior High:		
Lot shape:		High:		
Room Size Information		**Organization Information**		
Living room: Approx. _____ x _____ feet		☐ Planned Development ☐ Condominium		
Dining room: Approx. _____ x _____ feet		☐ Pool ☐ Spa		
Kitchen: Approx. _____ x _____ feet		☐ Tennis ☐ Golf		
Family room: Approx. _____ x _____ feet		☐ Rec room ☐ Other:		
Den: Approx. _____ x _____ feet		Homeowner's fees	$	
Bedroom 1: Approx. _____ x _____ feet		Maintenance	$	
Bedroom 2: Approx. _____ x _____ feet		Water/sewer	$	
Bedroom 3: Approx. _____ x _____ feet		Trash	$	
Bedroom 4: Approx. _____ x _____ feet		Insurance	$	
Bedroom 5: Approx. _____ x _____ feet		**Utility Information**		
Attic: Approx. _____ x _____ feet		☐ Sewer ☐ Septic tank ☐ Cesspool		
Garage: Approx. _____ x _____ feet		Heating type:		
Other: Approx. _____ x _____ feet		Television: ☐ Antenna ☐ Cable		
Amenities		Dryer hookup: ☐ Electric ☐ Gas		
☐ Patio ☐ Deck		**Appliances Included** ☐ Refrigerator		
☐ Pool ☐ Spa		☐ Stove ☐ Dishwasher		
☐ Fence ☐ Sprinklers		☐ Oven ☐ Disposal		
☐ View:		☐ Microwave ☐ Washer		
		☐ Trash compactor ☐ Dryer		

HOME INSPECTOR QUESTIONS WORKSHEET

Home inspector:_____ Telephone:_____

Address:_____

Ask	Question	Answer
	What are your credentials?	
	Are you a licensed home inspector?	☐ Yes ☐ No
	For how long have you been doing home inspections?	
	What do you charge for a home inspection?	$
	On what items do you report in the inspection?	
	Do you report on items in good condition?	☐ Yes ☐ No
	Do you report on items that are not currently problems but	☐ Yes ☐ No
	that may need repair or replacement in the next few years?	
	Do you have a vested interest in my property?	☐ Yes ☐ No
	What repairs are needed to my property?	
	Which repairs do you feel would be most cost-effective when	
	I sell?	
	Names & addresses of persons you recommend for	
	_____ repair?	
	Names & addresses of persons you recommend for	
	_____ repair?	
	Names & addresses of persons you recommend for	
	_____ repair?	
	Names & addresses of persons you recommend for	
	_____ repair?	
	Names & phone numbers of appraisers you recommend?	
	Names & phone numbers of geological inspectors you	
	recommend?	
	Names & phone numbers of pest control operators you	
	recommend?	

LENDER QUESTIONS WORKSHEET

Lender:_____ Telephone:_____

Address:_____

Ask	Question	Answer
	Do you mind answering my questions?	☐ Yes ☐ No
	How much do I owe on my loan?	$
	Does my loan have a prepayment penalty?	☐ Yes ☐ No
	If yes, how much is the prepayment penalty?	$
	Is my loan assumable?	☐ Yes ☐ No
	If yes, do you charge an assumption fee?	☐ Yes ☐ No
	If yes, how much is the assumption fee?	$
	If yes, do you require that you qualify buyers?	☐ Yes ☐ No
	If yes, do you require that you renegotiate the loan with buyers who want to assume my loan?	☐ Yes ☐ No
	If yes, will you release me from liability if the buyers assume my loan?	☐ Yes ☐ No
	Is my loan a "subject-to" loan?	☐ Yes ☐ No
	Is my loan due on sale?	☐ Yes ☐ No
	Would you approve a lease option?	☐ Yes ☐ No
	Names & phone numbers of appraisers you recommend?	
	Will you prequalify my buyers?	☐ Yes ☐ No
	Will you make a loan commitment in writing?	☐ Yes ☐ No
	Will you approve a bridge loan?	☐ Yes ☐ No
	Must buyers get a new first loan?	☐ Yes ☐ No
	Who usually pays closing/escrow fees?	
	Your cost estimate for an appraisal fee?	$
	Your cost estimate for an assumption fee?	$
	Your cost estimate for beneficiary statement?	$
	Your cost estimate for closing/escrow fees?	$
	Your cost estimate for credit report fee?	$
	Your cost estimate for delinquent payments on my account?	$
	Your cost estimate for demand fee?	$
	Your cost estimate for impounds?	$
	Your cost estimate for interest?	$
	Your cost estimate for a loan tie-in fee?	$
	Your cost estimate for a loan origination fee?	$
	Your cost estimate for points?	$
	Your cost estimate for a prepayment penalty?	$
	Do I have your permission for a buyer to assume a second loan?	☐ Yes ☐ No
	Do I have your permission for a buyer to take title subject to?	☐ Yes ☐ No
	Do you require a loan escrow to make a loan?	☐ Yes ☐ No
	Is standard coverage title insurance required?	☐ Yes ☐ No

(continued)

LENDER QUESTIONS WORKSHEET

Lender:_____   Telephone:_____

Address:_____

Ask	Question	Answer
	Is extended coverage title insurance required?	☐ Yes ☐ No
	Who usually pays the title insurance fee?	
	Is a pest control inspection and report required?	☐ Yes ☐ No
	Names & phone numbers of sellers of home protection plans you recommend?	
	Who pays notary fees?	
	Is escrow a condition of making a loan?	☐ Yes ☐ No
	When will your appraiser come to evaluate my property?	
	Will you give me a written loan committment?	☐ Yes ☐ No
	Do you require a statement of the impound account?	☐ Yes ☐ No
	Do you require a copy of the reconveyance deed?	☐ Yes ☐ No

NET PROCEEDS WORKSHEET

Name:_____ Date:_____

Address:_____

Costs Calculations	
Mortgage Costs	
First mortgage/trust deed (TD)	
First mortgage/trust deed prepayment penalty	
Second mortgage/trust deed (TD)	
Second mortgage/trust deed prepayment penalty	
Third mortgage/trust deed (TD)	
Third mortgage/trust deed prepayment penalty	
Marketing Costs	
Improvement costs	
Repair costs	
Attractiveness costs	
Advertising costs	
Other costs:	
Closing Costs	
Moving Costs	
TOTAL Costs	

Net Proceeds Calculation	
Asking Price	
- Total Costs	
= **Net Proceeds**	

OWNERSHIP COSTS WORKSHEET

Name:_____   Date:_____

Address:_____

Year	Month	Electric	Gas/Oil	Water	Sewer	Trash		Utilities Subtotal
	January							
	February							
	March							
	April							
	May							
	June							
	July							
	August							
	September							
	October							
	November							
	December							
Total								
Number of months								
Average/month								

Year	Month	Assn. dues	Insur-ance	Taxes		Other Subtotal	Grand Total
	January						
	February						
	March						
	April						
	May						
	June						
	July						
	August						
	September						
	October						
	November						
	December						
Total							
Number of months							
Average/month							

PROPERTY RECORDS WORKSHEET

Name: _____

Address: _____

Find	Copy	File	Description	Notes
			Purchase documentation	
			Closing statement	
			Conditions, covenants, &	
			restrictions (CC&Rs)	
			Deed	
			Physical inspection report	
			Geological inspection report	
			Pest control inspection report	
			Title insurance	
			Other:	
			Insurance documentation	
			Fire	
			Homeowner's	
			Mortgage	
			Other:	
			Loan documentation	
			Mortgage	
			Trust deed	
			Promissory note	
			Payment statements	
			Property tax statements	
			Assessment notices	
			Improvement notices	
			Satisfaction of mortgage(s)	
			Reconveyance deed(s)	
			Other:	
			Maintenance records	
			Item:	
			Invoices	
			Guarantees & warranties	
			Other:	
			Item:	
			Invoices	
			Guarantees & warranties	
			Other:	

(continued)

PROPERTY RECORDS WORKSHEET

Name: _____

Address: _____

Find	Copy	File	Description	Notes
			Maintenance records	
			Item:	
			Invoices	
			Guarantees & warranties	
			Other:	
			Item:	
			Invoices	
			Guarantees & warranties	
			Other:	
			Improvement documentation	
			Improvement:	
			Plans & specifications	
			Estimates	
			Contracts	
			Building permits	
			Inspection records	
			Payment records	
			Invoices	
			Preliminary lien notices	
			Completion notices	
			Lien releases	
			Other:	
			Improvement:	
			Plans & specifications	
			Estimates	
			Contracts	
			Building permits	
			Inspection records	
			Payment records	
			Invoices	
			Preliminary lien notices	
			Completion notices	
			Lien releases	
			Other:	

REAL ESTATE PROFESSIONAL QUESTIONS WORKSHEET

RE professional:_____ Telephone:_____

Address:_____

Ask	Question	Answer
	What are your credentials?	
	How many transactions do you handle per year?	
	Do you mind answering my questions?	☐ Yes ☐ No
	Will you provide a market evaluation at no cost or obligation?	☐ Yes ☐ No
	What are the prices of comparable properties in the neighborhood?	
	Names & phone numbers of appraisers you recommend?	
	Names & phone numbers of closing agents you recommend?	
	Names & phone numbers of escrow holders you recommend?	
	Names & phone numbers of home inspectors you recommend?	
	Names & phone numbers of pest control operators you recommend?	
	Names & phone numbers of title companies you recommend?	
	Do you consult?	☐ Yes ☐ No
	If yes, how much do you charge per hour for consulting?	$
	If yes, will you review a contract for me?	☐ Yes ☐ No
	If I sign a one-time permission to show, will you show my property?	☐ Yes ☐ No
	Will you submit my listing to the MLS for a fee?	☐ Yes ☐ No
	If yes, what is the fee?	$
	What services do you provide for a discounted commission?	
	What sign laws should I be aware of in this community?	
	What laws regarding discrimination apply to this sale?	
	What laws regarding disclosure apply to this sale?	
	Is a pest control inspection necessary by law?	☐ Yes ☐ No
	If yes, who must pay?	
	Is a physical inspection necessary by law?	☐ Yes ☐ No
	If yes, who must pay?	
	What marketing ideas do you suggest I consider?	
	What financing ideas do you suggest I consider?	
	Do you suggest I use an escrow?	☐ Yes ☐ No
	If yes, for how long do you suggest that the escrow last?	
	Who do you recommend pay the title insurance fees?	
	Who do you recommend pay the transfer tax on this sale?	
	What date do you suggest buyers take possession?	
	Do you suggest that I have a physical inspection done?	☐ Yes ☐ No
	Do you suggest that I have a geological inspection done?	☐ Yes ☐ No
	Is Flood Hazard Area Disclosure required?	☐ Yes ☐ No

(continued)

REAL ESTATE PROFESSIONAL QUESTIONS WORKSHEET

RE professional:_____   Telephone:_____

Address:_____

Ask	Question	Answer
	Is disclosure for earthquake potential required?	☐ Yes ☐ No
	What regulations apply regarding smoke detectors?	
	Your cost estimate for an appraisal fee?	$
	Your cost estimate for an assumption fee?	$
	Your cost estimate for beneficiary statement?	$
	Your cost estimate for closing/escrow fees?	$
	Your cost estimate for credit report fee?	$
	Your cost estimate for deliquent payments on my account?	$
	Your cost estimate for demand fee?	$
	Your cost estimate for document preparation fees?	$
	Your cost estimate for drawing deed fees?	$
	Your cost estimate for hazard insurance costs?	$
	Your cost estimate for home warranty costs?	$
	Your cost estimate for impounds?	$
	Your cost estimate for interest?	$
	Your cost estimate for a loan origination fee?	$
	Your cost estimate for a loan tie-in fee?	$
	Your cost estimate for notary fees?	$
	Your cost estimate for pest control inspection fees?	$
	Who usually pays pest control inspection fees?	
	Your cost estimate for physical inspection fees?	$
	Who usually pays physical inspection fees?	
	Your cost estimate for points?	$
	Your cost estimate for a prepayment penalty?	$
	Your cost estimate for a reconveyance deed?	$
	Your cost estimate for a recording fee?	$
	Your cost estimate for satisfaction of mortgage fee?	$
	Your cost estimate for the title search fee?	$
	Your cost estimate for the title insurance?	$
	Your cost estimate for the transfer fee?	$
	Your cost estimate for the transfer tax?	$
	What are the results of the preliminary title report?	
	Which of the items on the report might prevent closing?	
	How do you recommend I handle these items?	

REPAIRS WORKSHEET

Name:_____   Date:_____

Address:_____

Jobs to Be Done						
Do	By	Date	Job Description	Contractor & phone number *or* Material needed	Cost Estimate	Did
			Lawn			
			Bare spots replanted			
			Lawn fertilized			
			Other:			
			Plantings			
			Dead/ill parts removed			
			Dead/ill plants removed			
			Dead/ill plants replaced			
			Other:			
			Driveways and Walks			
			Holes patched			
			Asphalt sealed			
			Gravel smoothed			
			Other:			
			Walls and Fences			
			Sections repaired			
			Sections painted			
			Termite & rot free			
			Other:			
			Pools and Spas			
			Free of algae			
			Motor works			
			Filter works			
			Pool cleaner works			
			Cover in good repair			
			Other:			
			Septic Tanks/Leach Lines			
			Drain away from house			
			Area dry			
			Area odorless			
			Other:			
				Subtotal #1		

(continued)

REPAIRS WORKSHEET

Name:_____ Date:_____

Address:_____

Jobs to Be Done						
Do	By	Date	Job Description	Contractors & phone number *or* Material needed	Cost Estimate	Did
			Roof			
			Missing parts replaced			
			Broken parts repaired			
			Flashing leak free			
			Other:			
			Gutters			
			Missing sections replaced			
			Broken sections repaired			
			Gutters cleaned			
			Drains away from house			
			Other:			
			Siding and Walls			
			Missing parts replaced			
			Broken parts repaired			
			Cracks repaired			
			Painted			
			Other:			
			Foundation			
			Cracks repaired			
			Painted			
			Other:			
			Patios			
			Sections repaired			
			Sections painted			
			Termite & rot free			
			Other:			
			Decks			
			Stained or painted			
			Termite & rot free			
			Railing sturdy			
			Other:			
				Subtotal #2		

(continued)

REPAIRS WORKSHEET

Name:_____   Date:_____

Address:_____

Jobs to Be Done						
Do	By	Date	Job Description	Contractor & phone number *or* Material needed	Cost Estimate	Did
			Windows			
			Awnings in good repair			
			Awnings hung properly			
			Shutters in good repair			
			Shutters hung properly			
			Screens present			
			Screens in good repair			
			Panes in good repair			
			Sashes painted			
			Storm windows secure			
			Storm windows caulked			
			Other:			
			Entrance			
			Ceiling painted			
			Lights work			
			Walls repaired			
			Walls painted			
			Steps repaired			
			Steps painted			
			Doorbell works			
			Door painted or oiled			
			Doors work			
			Woodwork painted			
			Rugs or mats secure			
			Floor repaired			
			Closets repaired			
			Closets painted			
			Other:			
			Chimney			
			Straight			
			Bricks all present			
			Bricks mortared tight			
			Other:			
				Subtotal #3		

(continued)

REPAIRS WORKSHEET

Name:_____Date:_____

Address:_____

Jobs to Be Done						
Do	By	Date	Job Description	Contractor & phone number *or* Material needed	Cost Estimate	Did
			Kitchen			
			Ceiling painted			
			Lights work			
			Walls repaired			
			Walls painted/papered			
			Window hardware works			
			Counters repaired			
			Disposal works			
			Stove works			
			Hood works			
			Oven works			
			Microwave works			
			Trash compactor works			
			Cupboards repaired			
			Floor repaired			
			Other:			
			Utilities			
			Air conditioner works			
			Dryer works			
			Heating system works			
			Intercom works			
			Security systems works			
			Smoke detectors work			
			Washer works			
			Water heater works			
			Water softener works			
			Other			
			Garage or Carport			
			Roof free of leaks			
			Garage door balanced			
			Door opener works			
			Doors work/painted			
			Windows work			
			Lights work			
			Other:			
				Subtotal #4		

(continued)

REPAIRS WORKSHEET

Name:_____ Date:_____

Address:_____

			Jobs to Be Done			
Do	By	Date	Job Description	Contractor & phone number *or* Material needed	Cost Estimate	Did
			Room:			
			Ceiling painted			
			Lights work			
			Lights cleaned			
			Walls repaired			
			Walls painted			
			Wallpaper tight			
			Windows work easily			
			Window coverings clean			
			Drapery hardware works			
			Woodwork painted			
			Doors painted or oiled			
			Door hardware repaired			
			Heater works			
			Fireplace repaired			
			Floor repaired			
			Carpet repaired			
			Other:			
			Bedroom #:			
			Ceiling painted			
			Lights work			
			Lights cleaned			
			Walls repaired			
			Walls painted			
			Wallpaper tight			
			Windows work easily			
			Window coverings clean			
			Drapery hardware works			
			Woodwork painted			
			Doors painted or oiled			
			Door hardware repaired			
			Heater works			
			Fireplace repaired			
			Floor repaired			
			Carpet repaired			
			Other:			
			Subtotal #			

(continued)

REPAIRS WORKSHEET

Name:_____Date:_____

Address:_____

			Jobs to Be Done			
Do	By	Date	Job Description	Contractor & phone number *or* Material needed	Cost Estimate	Did
			Bathroom #:			
			Ceiling painted			
			Lights work			
			Heater works			
			Exhaust fan works			
			Walls repaired			
			Walls painted/papered			
			Windows work			
			Cabinet hardware works			
			Door hardware repaired			
			Woodwork painted			
			Tiles repaired/caulked			
			Sink works/repaired			
			Toilet works			
			Bath works/repaired			
			Flooring repaired			
			Other:			
				Subtotal #		

Subtotal # 1	
Subtotal # 2	
Subtotal # 3	
Subtotal # 4	
Subtotal #	
Subtotal #	
Subtotal #	
Subtotal #	
Subtotal #	
Subtotal #	
Subtotal #	
Subtotal #	
TOTAL	

STOP & START SERVICES WORKSHEET

Name:_____Effective date:_____

Old address:_____

New address:_____

	Call	Service	Name	Telephone	Did
S T O P		Cleaner			
		Dairy delivery			
		Diaper service			
		Drinking water			
		Fuel oil			
		Garbage/trash pickup			
		Gas			
		Landscaping service			
		Laundry service			
		Maid			
		Newspaper			
		Pest Control			
		Pool			
		Sewer			
		Telephone			
		Water			
		Water softener			
		Other:			
S T A R T		Cleaner			
		Dairy delivery			
		Diaper service			
		Drinking water			
		Fuel oil			
		Garbage/trash pickup			
		Gas			
		Landscaping service			
		Laundry service			
		Maid			
		Newspaper			
		Pest Control			
		Pool			
		Sewer			
		Telephone			
		Water			
		Water softener			
		Other:			

TELEPHONE REGISTER

Name: _____

Address: _____

Telephone: _____

Date	Ad Method	Name	Telephone Number	Appointment		Notes
				Date	Time	

TELEPHONE SCREENING CONVERSATION WORKSHEET

Name:_____ Telephone:_____

Address:_____

Use This Wording	Then
Hello! My name is _____. Thank you for calling. To whom am I speaking?	*Listen.*
Where did you hear about my property?	*Listen.*
What particularly interested you about my ad?	*Listen.*
My property is in the _____ section of _____ (city). Where do you live?	*Listen.*
My property has ____ bedrooms, _____ baths, and about _____ square feet of living space. Do you have a home now?	*Listen.*
My property also has the following (list important features): _____, _____, _____, _____, and _____. The price of our home is $_____. Are you looking for a home like this?	*Listen. If caller says no, thank him or her and hang up. If caller says yes, proceed.*
When may I set up an appointment for you to see the house?	*Listen. Whether the caller or you suggest a time, continue.*
That time sounds fine with me, but I must check with (others in family, my time manager) to be sure that there are no conflicts. I will call you back within the next _____ minutes. May I have your name and number?	*Listen. Say goodbye, then check for conflicts. (Even if you do not need to check for conflicts, do this. People are more likely to give you information this way.)* *Call the person back and set up an appointment.*

TITLE COMPANY QUESTIONS WORKSHEET

Title Co.:_____   Telephone:_____

Address:_____

Ask	Question	Answer
	Why should I use your services?	
	What is your charge for comparables?	$
	What are the sales prices of comparable properties in my neighborhood?	$
	What do you charge for a title survey?	$
	Will you work with me?	☐ Yes ☐ No
	Names and phone numbers of appraisers you recommend?	
	Names and phone numbers of closing agents you recommend?	
	Names and phone numbers of home inspectors you recommend?	
	Names and phone numbers of lenders you recommend?	
	Names and phone numbers of real estate professionals you recommend?	
	Your cost estimate for judgments against me?	$
	Your cost estimate for subescrow fee?	$
	Your cost estimate for title search fee?	$
	Your cost estimate for standard coverage title insurance?	$
	Your cost estimate for extended coverage title insurance?	$
	Your cost estimate for special endorsements?	$
	What are the results of the preliminary title report?	
	Which of the items might prevent closing?	
	How do you suggest I handle these items?	

WALK-THROUGH INSPECTION WORKSHEET

This walk-through inspection of the property known as _____

_____ on the date of _____

was conducted by _____ (seller)

and _____ (buyer).

1. Initial under **OK** for items that appear in satisfactory condition.
2. Check under **Fix** if the item needs to be handled and under Notes write what needs to be done.

OK	Fix	Item	Notes
		Outside	
		Deck	
		Driveway	
		Fences	
		Lawn	
		Leach lines	
		Low voltage lighting	
		Outdoor electrical	
		Patio	
		Plantings	
		Pool	
		Septic tank	
		Shed	
		Spa	
		Sprinklers	
		Walks	
		Walls	
		Well	
		Well pump	
		Other:	
		House Exterior	
		Roof	
		Gutters	
		Siding/walls	
		Foundation	
		Windows	
		Chimney	
		Other:	

(continued)

Buyer and seller acknowledge receiving a duplicate of this page, which is page 1 of ____ pages.

Buyers' initials (_____) (_____)   Sellers' initials (_____) (_____)

WALK-THROUGH INSPECTION WORKSHEET

Walk-through inspection of the property known as _____
_____ on the date of _____

OK	Fix	Item	Notes
		Room:	
		Ceiling	
		Electric	
		Floor	
		Hardware	
		Walls	
		Windows & coverings	
		Room:	
		Ceiling	
		Electric	
		Floor	
		Hardware	
		Walls	
		Windows & coverings	
		Bedroom #:	
		Ceiling	
		Electric	
		Floor	
		Hardware	
		Walls	
		Windows & coverings	
		Bathroom #:	
		Cabinets	
		Ceiling	
		Counter	
		Electric	
		Floor	
		Hardware	
		Showner/tub	
		Sink	
		Toilet	
		Walls	
		Windows & coverings	

(continued)

Buyer and seller acknowledge receiving a duplicate of this page, which is page ____ of ____ pages.
Buyers' initials (_____) (_____)   Sellers' initials (_____) (_____)

WALK-THROUGH INSPECTION WORKSHEET

Walk-through inspection of the property known as _____
_____ on the date of _____

OK	Fix	Item	Notes
		Kitchen	
		Ceiling	
		Counters	
		Cupboards	
		Dishwasher	
		Electric	
		Floor & floor coverings	
		Hardware	
		Oven & microwave	
		Range & hood	
		Sink(s) & disposal	
		Walls	
		Windows & coverings	
		Utilities	
		Heating system	
		Air-conditioning system	
		Smoke detector(s)	
		Water heater	
		Water softener	
		Central vacuum	
		Security system	
		Washer & dryer outlets	
		Garage	
		Built-in items	
		Ceiling	
		Electric	
		Floor	
		Garage door	
		Hardware	
		Walls	
		Windows & coverings	

Date:_____   Seller: _____
Date:_____   Seller: _____
Date:_____   Buyer: _____
Date:_____   Buyer: _____

Buyer and seller acknowledge receiving a duplicate of this page, which is page ____ of ____ pages.
Buyers' initials (_____) (_____)   Sellers' initials (_____) (_____)

CONDITION(S) RELEASE

This is meant to be a legally binding agreement. Read it carefully.

This addition is a part of the Purchase Contract for Real Estate and Deposit Receipt that is dated
_____between _____(seller)
and _____(buyer) on the property known as
_____ .

Seller has the right to continue to offer subject property for sale.

If the seller accepts a later written offer, in accordance with the named buyer's rights, the buyer shall
have _____hours _____days following receiving notice to remove and renounce in writing the
following condition(s): _____

_____

_____

_____

_____

_____

_____

_____

In the event buyer shall fail to remove the condition(s) within the above time limit, the Purchase Contract
for Real Estate and Deposit Receipt and this agreement shall end and become voidable and the buyer's
deposit shall be returned to the buyer.

This Condition(s) Release shall be considered to have been received by buyer when buyer, or buyer's
agent, has received notice by delivery in person or by certified mail addressed to _____
_____ .

If notice is given by mail, the buyer has until 6:00 P.M. of the third day following the date of mailing
(unless the notice provides another time), to deliver to the seller the buyer's written agreement to remove
and void the condition(s).

The person or persons signing below acknowledge receiving a copy of this document.

RECEIPT FOR DELIVERY IN PERSON

Date:_____ Seller:_____

Date:_____ Seller:_____

Date:_____ Buyer: _____

Date:_____ Buyer: _____

Buyer and seller acknowledge receiving a duplicate of this page, which is page 1 of _____ pages.
Buyers' initials (_____) (_____)   Sellers' initials (_____) (_____)

CONTRACT CHANGES AND ADDITIONS

This is meant to be a legally binding agreement. Read it carefully.

The following changes and additions are united with and made a part of the Real Estate Purchase Contract and Receipt for Deposit that is dated _____

between _____ , the seller, and

_____ , the buyer, on the property

known as _____ .

The changes and additions are as follows:

_____
_____
_____
_____
_____
_____
_____
_____
_____
_____
_____
_____
_____
_____
_____
_____
_____
_____
_____
_____
_____
_____
_____
_____
_____
_____
_____
_____

Receipt of this notice is acknowledged:

Date:_____   Seller:_____

Date:_____   Seller:_____

Date:_____   Buyer:_____

Date:_____   Buyer:_____

Buyer and seller acknowledge receiving a duplicate of this page, which is page ____ of ____ pages.

Buyers' initials (_____) (_____)   Sellers' initials (_____) (_____)

COUNTEROFFER

This is meant to be a legally binding agreement. Read it carefully.

This counteroffer to the Real Estate Purchase Contract and Receipt for Deposit on the property known as _____ is dated _____. In this contract _____ is referred to as the buyer and _____ is referred to as the seller.

Seller accepts all of the conditions and terms in the agreement noted above with the following changes:

_____
_____
_____
_____
_____
_____
_____
_____
_____
_____
_____
_____
_____
_____
_____
_____
_____
_____
_____
_____

The seller retains the right to continue to offer the property described for sale. The seller also retains the right to agree to any offer acceptable to seller at any time before the personal acceptance by seller of a copy of this counteroffer, properly accepted and signed by the buyer. *Accept* as used in this document, includes delivery in person, by mail, or by facsimile.

If this counteroffer is not accepted on or before the date of _____ at _____ A.M./P.M., the counteroffer shall be considered canceled and the deposit shall be returned to the buyer. The seller's agreement to another offer shall cancel this counteroffer. This counteroffer and any addition or modification relating to it, including any photocopy or facsimile of it, may be signed in two or more duplicates, all of which will make up the same writing. Acceptance of a copy is acknowledged.

Date: _____   Seller: _____

Time: _____   Seller: _____

                                                                   (continued)

Buyer and seller acknowledge receiving a duplicate of this page, which is page 1 of _____ pages.

Buyers' initials (_____) (_____)   Sellers' initials (_____) (_____)

COUNTEROFFER

This is meant to be a legally binding agreement. Read it carefully.

Property known as_____

☐ The undersigned buyer accepts the above counteroffer without addition or modification, **OR**

☐ The undersigned buyer accepts the above counteroffer with the following additions or modifications:

If the following additions or modifications are not accepted and a copy properly accepted and signed is not personally delivered to the buyer or _____, the agent obtaining the offer, on or before _____ at _____A.M./P.M., the counteroffer shall be considered cancelled and the deposit shall be returned to the buyer. Acceptance of a copy is acknowledged.

_____
_____
_____
_____
_____
_____
_____
_____
_____
_____

Date:_____   Buyer:_____
Time:_____   Buyer:_____

Acceptance of a signed copy on_____ at _____ A.M./P.M. by seller is acknowledged.

IF BUYER MADE ADDITIONS OR MODIFICATIONS ABOVE, THE FOLLOWING IS REQUIRED:
Seller accepts buyer's additions or modifications to seller's counteroffer. The seller agrees to sell on the above terms and conditions. Seller acknowledges receipt of a copy.

Date:_____   Seller:_____
Time:_____   Seller:_____

Buyer and seller acknowledge receiving a duplicate of this page, which is page 2 of ____ pages.
Buyers' initials (_____) (_____)   Sellers' initials (_____) (_____)

NOTICE TO BUYER TO REMOVE CONDITION(S)

This is meant to be a legally binding agreement. Read it carefully.

In agreement with the Condition Release Addition to the Purchase Contract for Real Estate and Deposit Receipt which is dated _____, between _____(Seller) and _____(Buyer) on the property known as: _____ .

This notice is to notify you, the Buyer, that the Seller has accepted a written offer conditioned upon your (the Buyer's) rights to remove the conditions outlined in the Conditions Release Addition.

Under the terms of the Conditions Release Addition, you have until _____ at 6:00 PM to remove the indicated condition(s). If you, the Buyer, fail to remove these conditions within the above specified time limit, the Purchase Contract for Real Estate and Deposit Receipt and all the rights and obligations under this agreement shall end and become voidable and your deposit shall be returned to you.

Date:_____   Seller:_____

                               Seller:_____

RECEIPT FOR DELIVERY IN PERSON

The person or persons signing below acknowledge receiving a copy of this document.

Date:_____   Buyer: _____

                               Buyer: _____

Buyer and Seller acknowledge receiving a duplicate of this page which is page 1 of ____ pages.

Buyer's Initials (_____) (_____)   Seller's Initials (_____) (_____)

PURCHASE CONTRACT FOR REAL ESTATE AND DEPOSIT RECEIPT

This is meant to be a legally binding agreement. Read it carefully.

City:_____ State:_____ Date:_____

Received from _____, the buyer, the sum of $_____

shown by ☐ cash, ☐ cashier's check, ☐ personal check, or ☐ _____

payable to _____

to be held uncashed until this offer is accepted as deposit toward the purchase price of

_____ Dollars ($_____)

for the purchase of property located in the state of _____,

county of _____, city of_____,

and known as _____.

CAPTIONS: The headings and captions in this document are to make reference easy and are not intended as a part of this agreement.

1. **FIXTURES:** All permanently installed fixtures, fittings, and plantings that are attached to the property or for which special openings were made, as well as their controls, if any, are included in the purchase price, including _____

    _____

    except _____.

2. **PERSONAL PROPERTY:** The following items of personal property, free of liens and without warranty are included: _____

    _____

3. **PROPERTY CONDITION:** Seller guarantees, that through the date seller makes possession available to buyer

    A. The property and improvements, including grounds and landscaping, shall be maintained in the same condition as on the date of acceptance of the offer;

    B. The roof is free of all known leaks;

    C. All permanently installed fixtures and fittings, as well as their controls, if any, are operative;

    D. Seller shall replace any cracked or broken glass;

    E. And _____

    F. Except _____

    _____

4. **SELLER REPRESENTATION:** Seller guarantees that until the date escrow closes that seller knows of no violation notices of codes, laws, or other regulations issued or filed against the property.

5. **SUPPLEMENTS:** The attached documents are incorporated in this document:

    ☐ _____

    ☐ _____

    ☐ _____

    ☐ _____

    (continued)

Buyer and seller acknowledge receiving a duplicate of this page, which is page 1 of ____ pages.

Buyers' initials (_____) (_____)   Sellers' initials (_____) (_____)

PURCHASE CONTRACT FOR REAL ESTATE AND DEPOSIT RECEIPT

Property known as _____

6. **ESCROW:** Buyer and seller shall deliver signed instructions to _____
_____, the escrow holder, within _____ calendar days of
acceptance of the offer. The offer shall provide for closing within _____ calendar days of acceptance.
Escrow fees to be paid as follows: _____
_____

7. **OCCUPANCY:** Buyer ☐ does   ☐ does not intend to occupy property as buyer's primary
residence.

8. **POSSESSION:** Possession and occupancy shall be delivered to buyer ☐ on the close of escrow
☐ no later than _____ days after the close of escrow or ☐ _____

9. **KEYS:** Seller shall provide keys and/or other means to operate all property locks and alarms, if any,
when possession is available to the buyer.

10. **FINANCING:** This agreement depends on the buyer obtaining financing.
    A. DILIGENCE AND GOOD FAITH - Buyer agrees to act with diligence and
       good faith to obtain all appropriate financing.
    B. DEPOSIT is due on acceptance and is to be deposited into _____
       _____ in the amount of $_____
    C. INCREASED DEPOSIT is due within _____ days of acceptance and is to be
       deposited into _____ in the amount of $_____
    D. DOWN PAYMENT BALANCE is to be deposited into _____
       _____ on or before _____ in the amount of $_____
    E. NEW FIRST LOAN - Buyer to apply for, qualify for, and obtain new first loan
       in the amount of .... $_____
       payable monthly at approximately $_____
       including interest at origination not to exceed _____ %
       ☐ fixed rate   ☐ other _____
       all due _____ years from the date of origination.
       Loan fee at origination not to exceed $_____ .
       Seller agrees to pay a maximum of _____ FHA/VA discount points.
       Additional terms:_____
       _____
       _____

    F. EXISTING FIRST LOAN - Buyer to ☐ assume   ☐ take title subject to
       an existing first loan with an approximate balance of .... $_____
       payable monthly at $_____ including interest at _____ %
       ☐ fixed rate   ☐ other _____
       Fees not to exceed $_____ . Disposition of impound account ___
       Additional terms: _____
       _____
       _____

(continued)

Buyer and seller acknowledge receiving a duplicate of this page, which is page 2 of ____ pages.
Buyers' initials (_____) (_____)   Sellers' initials (_____) (_____)

PURCHASE CONTRACT FOR REAL ESTATE AND DEPOSIT RECEIPT

Property known as _____

10. FINANCING:

   G. NOTE SECURED BY TRUST DEED - Buyer to sign a note secured by a
      ☐ first   ☐ second   ☐ third trust deed in the amount of .... $_____
      in favor of seller, payable monthly at $_____ or more
      including interest at _____ %
      ☐ fixed rate   ☐ other _____
      all due ☐ _____ years from date of origination or ☐ upon sale or
      transfer of the property.
      A late charge of $_____ shall be due on any installment not paid
      within _____ days of the date due.
      Additional terms: _____
      _____ .

   H. NEW SECOND LOAN - Buyer to apply for, qualify for, and obtain new
      second loan in the amount of .... $ _____
      payable monthly at approximately $_____
      including interest at origination not to exceed _____ %
      ☐ fixed rate   ☐ other _____
      all due _____ years from date of origination.
      Buyer's loan fees not to exceed $_____ .
      Seller agrees to pay a maximum of _____ FHA/VA discount points.
      Additional terms:_____
      _____ .

   I. EXISTING SECOND LOAN - Buyer to ☐ assume   ☐ take title subject
      to an existing second loan with an approximate balance of .... $_____
      payable monthly at $_____ including interest at _____ %
      ☐ fixed rate   ☐ other _____
      Buyers loan fees not to exceed $_____ .
      Additional terms:_____
      _____ .

   J. OTHER PROVISIONS - If buyer assumes or takes title "subject to" an existing
      loan, seller shall provide buyer with copies of applicable notes and trust deeds.
      Buyer is allowed _____ calendar days after receipt of such copies to
      examine the copies for the features that affect the loan and to notify seller in
      writing of disapproval. Buyer shall not unreasonably withhold approval.
      Failure to notify seller in writing shall conclusively be considered approval.

   K. ADDITIONAL FINANCING TERMS: _____
      _____
      _____

   L. TOTAL PURCHASE PRICE.. $_____

                                                        (continued)

Buyer and seller acknowledge receiving a duplicate of this page, which is page 3 of ____ pages.
              Buyers' initials (_____) (_____)   Sellers' initials (_____) (_____)

PURCHASE CONTRACT FOR REAL ESTATE AND DEPOSIT RECEIPT

Property known as _____

11. **TITLE:** Title is to be free of conditions, easements, encumbrances, liens, restrictions, and rights of record other than the following:

   A.   Current property taxes;

   B.   Covenants, conditions, restrictions, and public utility easements of record, if any, if the items do not adversely affect the continuing use of the property for the purposes for which it is currently used, unless the buyer reasonably disapproves in writing within _____ calendar days of receipt of a current preliminary report furnished at _____ expense; and

   C.   Seller shall furnish buyer at _____ expense, a _____ policy issued by _____ company, showing title vested in buyer subject only to the above. If seller is unwilling or unable to eliminate any title matter disapproved by buyer as indicated above, the buyer may end this agreement. If seller fails to deliver title as indicated above, buyer may end this agreement. In either case deposit shall be returned to the buyer.

12. **VESTING:** The title shall vest as follows: _____ _____ unless noted otherwise in the buyer's escrow instructions.

13. **PRORATIONS:** Association dues, interest, payments on assessments and bonds assumed by buyer, premiums on insurance acceptable to the buyer, property taxes, rents, and _____ _____ shall be paid current and prorated as of

   ☐ the day the deed records; or ☐ _____ .
   Bonds or assessments that are now a lien shall be paid current by seller, payments not yet due to be

   ☐ assumed by the buyer; ☐ paid in full by the seller, including payments not yet due; or

   ☐ _____ .
   County transfer tax, if applicable, shall be paid by _____ . The _____ transfer tax or transfer fee shall be paid by _____ . Reassessment of the property when ownership changes affects taxes to be paid.   A supplemental tax bill may be issued, which shall be paid by the seller for periods before escrow closes and by the buyer for periods after escrow closes. Buyer and seller shall handle between themselves tax bills issued after escrow closes.

14. **TAX WITHHOLDING:** Under the Foreign Investment in Real Property Tax Act (FIRPTA), buyers of U.S. real property *must* deduct and withhold from the seller's proceeds 10% of the gross sales price unless an exemption applies. States may require that additional money be withheld.

15. **OTHER TERMS AND CONDITIONS:**

   _____
   _____
   _____
   _____
   _____
   _____
   _____
   _____

16. **ATTORNEY'S FEES:** In any action, arbitration, or proceeding arising out of this agreement, the prevailing party shall be entitled to reasonable attorney's fees and costs.

(continued)

Buyer and seller acknowledge receiving a duplicate of this page, which is page 4 of ____ pages.

Buyers' initials (_____) (_____)   Sellers' initials (_____) (_____)

PURCHASE CONTRACT FOR REAL ESTATE AND DEPOSIT RECEIPT

Property known as _____

17. ENTIRE CONTRACT:
   A. Time is important.
   B. All earlier agreements between buyer and seller are made a part of this agreement, which makes up the whole contract. The terms of this contract are intended by buyer and seller as their final agreement about the terms that are included in this contract. The terms of this contract may not be contradicted by evidence of any earlier agreement or any oral contract made at the same time as this written contract.
   C. The buyer and seller agree that this contract makes up the complete and exclusive statement of the contract's terms and that no extraneous evidence of any kind may be introduced in any judicial or arbitration proceeding, if any, about this contract.

18. AMENDMENTS:

The buyer and seller may not alter, amend, change, or modify this contract except by further agreement in writing signed by both buyer and seller.

19. OFFER:
   A. This makes up an offer to purchase the property described.
   B. Unless acceptance is signed by seller and a signed copy is delivered in person, by mail, or facsimile and received by the buyer at the address indicated below within _____ calendar days of the date of this contract, this offer will be considered revoked and the deposit shall be returned.
   C. Buyer has read and acknowledges receipt of a copy of this offer.
   D. This agreement and any addition or modification relating to this agreement including any photocopy or facsimile of this contract may be signed in two or more counterparts, all of which shall make up one and the same writing.

BUYER:_____   BUYER:_____
Address:_____   Address:_____
_____   _____
Telephone:_____   Telephone:_____

ACCEPTANCE

The seller who signed below accepts and agrees to sell the property in the manner indicated below.
   ☐ On the above terms and conditions.   ☐ Subject to the attached counteroffer.

SELLER:_____   SELLER:_____
Address:_____   Address:_____
_____   _____
Telephone:_____   Telephone:_____

Buyer and Seller acknowledge receiving a duplicate of this page, which is page 5 of ____ pages.
Buyers' initials (_____) (_____)   Sellers' initials (_____) (_____)

PURCHASE CONTRACT FOR REAL ESTATE
ADDITIONAL TERMS AND CONDITIONS
This is meant to be a legally binding agreement. Read it carefully.

This document contains additional terms and conditions to the Purchase Contract for Real Estate and Deposit Receipt for the purchase of the property located in the state of_____,
county of _____ , city of _____,
and known as _____.
This document, when used, is meant to be an addition to the Purchase Contract for Real Estate and Deposit Receipt.

CAPTIONS: The headings and captions in this document are to make reference easy and are not
intended as a part of this agreement.

To be included in the agreement items *must* be initialed by both *buyer(s)* and *seller(s)*.

1. **PHYSICAL AND GEOLOGICAL INSPECTIONS:**
   A. Buyer has the right, at buyer's expense, to select a licensed contractor and /or other qualified professional(s) to make inspections of the property for possible environmental hazards.
   - These inspections can include inspections, investigations, tests, and other studies.
   - The inspections can include but are not limited to the fixtures and fittings of the property and controls for the fixtures and fittings, if any; geological conditions; and possible environmental hazards including substances, products, and other conditions.
   B. Buyer shall keep the property free and clear of any liens. Buyer shall indemnify and hold seller harmless from all liability, claims, demands, damages, or costs and shall repair all damages to the property arising from the inspections.
   C. Buyer shall make all claims about defects in the condition of the property that adversely affect continuing use of the property for the purposes for which it is currently being used or as _____ in writing, supported by written reports, if any.
   _____ The buyer shall cause these documents to be delivered to the seller, within the number of calendar days specified below of the acceptance of the offer.   For all types of physical inspections, except geological inspections, the documents shall be delivered within _____ calendar days.   For geological inspections the documents shall be delivered within _____ calendar days.
   D. Buyer shall provide seller with copies, at no cost to the seller, of all reports about the property obtained by the buyer.
   E. Buyer may cancel this agreement if any of these reports disclose conditions or information unacceptable to the buyer, which the seller is unable or unwilling to correct.
   F. Seller shall make the property available for all inspections.
   G. *Buyer's failure to notify seller in writing regarding the above shall conclusively be considered approval.*

   Initials: Buyers: _____ _____   Sellers: _____ _____
   (continued)

Buyer and seller acknowledge receiving a duplicate of this page, which is page 1 of ____ pages.
   Buyers' initials (_____) (_____)   Sellers' initials (_____) (_____)

PURCHASE CONTRACT FOR REAL ESTATE
ADDITIONAL TERMS AND CONDITIONS

Property known as _____

2. PEST CONTROL

A. Within _____ calendar days of acceptance of the offer, seller shall furnish buyer at the expense of ☐ buyer, ☐ seller, a current written report of an inspection by _____ _____, a licensed pest control operator. This inspection shall be of one or more of the following areas: ☐ the main building, ☐ detached garage(s) or carport(s), if any, and ☐ the following other structure(s) on the property:_____ _____.

B. If either Buyer or Seller request it, the report shall separately identify each recommendation for corrective action as follows:
Type 1: Infestation or infection that is evident.
Type 2: Conditions present that are considered likely to lead to infestation or infection.

C. If no infestation or infection by wood-destroying pests or organisms is found, the report shall include a written certification that on the inspection date no evidence of active infestation or infection was found.

D. All work recommended to correct conditions described as type 1 shall be at the expense of the ☐ seller. ☐ buyer.

E. All work recommended to correct conditions described as type 2, if requested by the buyer, shall be at the expense of the ☐ seller. ☐ buyer.

F. The repairs shall be done with good workmanship and materials of comparable quality to the originals. These repairs shall include repairs and the replacement of materials removed for repairs. Buyer and seller understand that exact restoration of appearance or cosmetic items following all such repairs is not included.

G. Funds for work agreed to be performed after escrow closes shall be held in escrow and paid on receipt of written certification that the inspected property is now free of active infestation or infection.

H. If the report recommends inspection of inaccessible areas, buyer has the option to accept and approve the report, or within _____ calendar days from receipt of the report to request in writing that a further inspection be made. *Buyer's failure to notify seller in writing of such request shall conclusively be considered approval of the report.*
If additional inspection recommends type 1 or 2 corrective measures, such work shall be done at the expense of whoever is designated in section 2D and/or 2E above. If no infestation is found, the cost of inspection, entry, and closing of inaccessible areas shall be at buyer's expense.

I. Other _____
_____
_____
_____
_____

Initials: Buyers: _____ _____   Sellers: _____ _____

(continued)

Buyer and seller acknowledge receiving a duplicate of this page, which is page 2 of ____ pages.
Buyers' initials (_____) (_____)   Sellers' initials (_____) (_____)

PURCHASE CONTRACT FOR REAL ESTATE
ADDITIONAL TERMS AND CONDITIONS

Property known as _____

3. ENERGY CONSERVATION RETROFIT:

If applicable, governmental laws require that the property be made to conform to minimum energy conservation standards as a condition of sale or transfer; ☐ buyer, ☐ seller shall comply with and pay for the work necessary to meet these requirements. If the seller must bring the property into compliance, the seller may, where the law permits, authorize escrow to credit the buyer with enough funds to cover the cost of the retrofit.

      Initials: Buyers: _____ _____   Sellers: _____ _____

4. FLOOD HAZARD AREA DISCLOSURE:

The buyer is informed that the property is located in a "Special Flood Hazard Area" as set forth on a Federal Emergency Management Agency (FEMA) "Flood Insurance Rate Map" (FIRM) or "Flood Hazard Boundary Map" (FHBM).

A. The law requires that, to obtain financing on most structures located in a "Special Flood Hazard Area," lenders require flood insurance where the property or its attachments are security for a loan.

B. No representation is made by the seller as to the legal or economic effects of the National Flood Insurance Program and related legislation.

      Initials: Buyers: _____ _____   Sellers: _____ _____

5. HOME PROTECTION PLAN:

Home protection plans may provide additional protection and benefit to seller and buyer.

The buyer and seller agree to include a home protection plan to be issued by _____

_____

at a cost not to exceed $_____ to be paid for by ☐ Buyer, ☐ Seller.

      Initials: Buyers: _____ _____   Sellers: _____ _____

6. CONDOMINIUM/PLANNED UNIT DEVELOPMENT (PUD):

A. The property is a ☐ condominium ☐ planned unit development (PUD) designated as unit _____ and _____ parking spaces, and an undivided interest in community areas, and

_____.

The current monthly assessment charge, fees, or dues by the homeowner's association or other governing body is $_____.

B. As soon as practical, seller shall provide buyer with copies of any documents required by law including the articles of incorporation; claims; covenants, conditions, and restrictions; current rules and regulations; litigations; most current financial statement; and pending special assessments.

C. Buyer is allowed _____ calendar days from receipt to review these documents. If documents disclose conditions or information unacceptable to buyer, buyer may cancel this agreement.

D. *Buyer's failure to notify seller in writing shall conclusively be considered approval.*

      Initials: Buyers: _____ _____   Sellers: _____ _____

(continued)

Buyer and seller acknowledge receiving a duplicate of this page, which is page 3 of ____ pages.

    Buyers' initials (_____) (_____)   Sellers' initials (_____) (_____)

PURCHASE CONTRACT FOR REAL ESTATE
ADDITIONAL TERMS AND CONDITIONS

Property known as _____

7. LIQUIDATED DAMAGES: If buyer fails to complete purchase of the property because of any default of the buyer, seller is released from obligation to sell the property to buyer. Seller may then proceed against buyer on any claim or remedy that seller may have in equity or law. By initialing this paragraph, buyer and seller agree that seller shall retain the deposit as liquidated damages.
NOTICE: Funds deposited in trust accounts or in escrow are not released automatically in the event of a dispute. Release of funds requires written agreement of the parties, judicial decision, or arbitration.

Initials: Buyers: _____ _____   Sellers: _____ _____

8. DISPUTE ARBITRATION: Any dispute or claim in law or equity arising out of this contract or any resulting transaction shall be decided by neutral binding arbitration in accordance with the rules of the American Arbitration Association and not by state law except as the law provides for judicial review of arbitration proceedings. Judgment upon the award rendered by the arbitrator shall be entered in any court having jurisdiction over the case. The parties shall have the right of discovery.
The following matters are excluded from arbitration:
A. A judicial or nonjudicial foreclosure or other action or proceeding to enforce a deed of trust, mortgage, or a real property sales contract.
B. An unlawful detainer action.
C. The filing or enforcement of a mechanic's lien.
D. Any matter that is within the jurisdiction of a probate court, and/or
E. Bodily injury, wrongful death, hidden or evident defects, and actions to which civil codes apply. The filing of a judicial action to enable the recording of a notice of pending action, for order of attachment, receivership, injunction, or other temporary remedies, shall not be a waiver of the right to arbitrate under this provision.
NOTICE: Agreement to this provision is voluntary. If you refuse to submit to arbitration after agreeing to this provision, you may be forced to arbitrate. By initialing below you are
A. Agreeing to have any dispute arising out of the matters included in this "Dispute Arbitration" provision decided by neutral arbitration as provided by your state law.
B. Giving up any rights you may possess to have the dispute litigated in a court or jury trial.
C. Giving up your judicial rights to discovery and appeal, unless those rights are specifically included in the "Dispute Arbitration" provision.
We have read and understood this provision to arbitrate a dispute, and we agree to this provision.

Initials: Buyers: _____ _____   Sellers: _____ _____

Receipt of this document is acknowledged:
Date:_____   Seller: _____
Date:_____   Seller: _____
Date:_____   Buyer: _____
Date:_____   Buyer: _____

Buyer and seller acknowledge receiving a duplicate of this page, which is page 4 of ____ pages.
Buyers' initials (_____) (_____)   Sellers' initials (_____) (_____)

REAL ESTATE DISCLOSURE STATEMENT

This declaration of the condition of the property described below is not intended to be a part of the contract between the buyer(s) and the seller(s). This declaration is not a warranty by the seller(s) and is not a replacement for any inspections or warranties the buyer(s) may want to obtain.

This declaration concerns the real property located in the state of _____,
county of _____, city of _____,
and known as _____.

SELLER'S INFORMATION

A. Occupancy
   The seller ☐ is ☐ is not occupying the property.

B. The property has the items checked below:

Has	Item	Has	Item	Has	Item
	Air conditioning, central		Gazebo		Spa
	Air conditioning, wall		Hot tub		Sprinklers
	Air conditioning, window		Intercom		Sump pump
	Barbecue (built-in)		Microwave		Trash compactor
	Carport		Oven		T.V. antenna
	Central heating, electric		Patio		Washer/dryer hookups
	Central heating, gas		Pool		Water heater, electric
	Central heating, solar		Pool/spa heater, electric		Water heater, gas
	Deck		Pool/spa heater, gas		Water heater, solar
	Dishwasher		Pool/spa heater, solar		Water softener
	Evaporative cooler(s)		Public sewer system		Water supply, city
	Fire alarm		Rain gutters		Water supply, private
	Garage, attached		Range		Water supply, well
	Garage, detached		Satellite dish		Water supply, other
	Garage door opener		Sauna		Window screens
	# of controls		Security gate		
	Garbage disposal		Security system		
	Gas supply, bottled		Septic tank		
	Gas supply, utility		Smoke detector(s)		

☐ 220 volt wiring in _____
☐ Exhaust fans in _____
☐ Fireplaces in _____
☐ Roof(s): Type(s):_____ Approximate age:_____
   Type(s):_____ Approximate age:_____
                                                          (continued)

Buyer and seller acknowledge receiving a duplicate of this page, which is page 1 of ____ pages.
   Buyers' initials (_____) (_____)   Sellers' initials (_____) (_____)

REAL ESTATE DISCLOSURE STATEMENT

SELLER'S INFORMATION

☐ To the best of my/our, the seller/sellers, knowledge all the above are in operating condition.

☐ To the best of my/our, the seller/sellers, knowledge all the above are in operating condition, except the items described below (or on additional sheets if necessary):

_____

_____

_____

_____

_____

_____

_____

_____

_____

_____

_____

_____

_____

C. ☐ I/We, the seller/sellers, are not aware of any significant malfunctions or defects in the following:

X	Item
	Ceilings
	Doors
	Driveways
	Electrical systems
	Exterior walls
	Floors
	Foundation
	Insulation

X	Item
	Interior walls
	Plumbing/sewer/septic systems
	Roofs
	Sidewalks
	Slab(s)
	Walls/fences
	Windows
	Other structural components

☐ I/We, the seller/sellers, are aware of significant malfunctions or defects in the items indicated by the *X* above. Descriptions and explanations of the problems follow (or are on additional sheets as necessary). Item(s), description(s), and explanation(s):_____

_____

_____

_____

_____

_____

_____

_____

_____

_____

_____

_____

(continued)

Buyer and seller acknowledge receiving a duplicate of this page, which is page 2 of ____ pages.

Buyers' initials (_____) (_____)   Sellers' initials (_____) (_____)

REAL ESTATE DISCLOSURE STATEMENT

SELLER'S INFORMATION

D.   I/we, the seller/sellers, are aware of the items indicated by the *X* below

X	Item
	1. Citations or abatement notices against the property.
	2. Common areas (co-owned in undivided interest with others (e.g., pool, spa, or tennis courts).
	3. Deed restrictions or other obligations including covenants, conditions, & restrictions (CC&Rs).
	4. Drainage, flooding, or grading problems.
	5. Encroachments, easements, and so forth that may affect my/our interest in the property.
	6. Features of property shared in common with adjoining landowners, whose use or responsibility for maintenance may affect the property (e.g., walls, fences, and driveways).
	7. Homeowner's association that has any authority over the property.
	8. Landfill (compacted or not compacted) on any part of the property.
	9. Lawsuits against the seller(s) that affect, or threaten to affect, the property.
	10. Major damage to the property or structures from earthquakes, fire, floods, or landslides.
	11. Neighborhood nuisances including noise problems.
	12. Nonconforming uses, setback requirement violations, or zoning violations.
	13. Room additions, structural alterations, or other modifications made without necessary permits.
	14. Room additions, structural alterations, or other modifications not complying with building codes.
	15. Soil problem from any cause (e.g., settling, slippage, or sliding).
	16. Substances, materials, or products that may be an environmental hazard on the property (Such as, but not limited to, asbestos, chemical or fuel storage tanks, contaminated soil or water, formaldehyde, lead-based paint, and/or radon gas).

Explanation(s):_____
_____
_____
_____
_____
_____
_____
_____
_____

The seller attests that the information in this document is true and correct to the best of the knowledge of the seller as of the date this document was signed by the seller.

Date:_____   Seller:_____

Date:_____   Seller: _____

The person or persons signing below acknowledge receiving a copy of this document.

Date:_____   Buyer: _____

Date:_____   Buyer: _____

Buyer and seller acknowledge receiving a duplicate of this page, which is page 3 of ____ pages.

Buyers' initials (_____) (_____)   Sellers' initials (_____) (_____)

Appendix

Deeds Chart

G = Grant deed is a deed using the word *grant* in the clause that awards ownership. This written document is used by the grantor (seller) to transfer title to the grantee (buyer). Grant deeds have two implied warranties. One is that the grantor has not previously transferred the title. The other is that the title is free from encumbrances that are not visible to the grantee. This deed also transfers any title acquired by the grantor after delivery of the deed.

W = Warranty deed is a deed in which the grantor (usually the seller) guarantees the title to be in the condition indicated in the deed. The grantor agrees to protect the grantee (usually the buyer) against all claimants to the property.

* = Special deed.

STATE	DEEDS	STATE	DEEDS	STATE	DEEDS
Alabama	W	Louisiana	W	Oklahoma	G
Alaska	W	Maine	W	Oregon	W
Arizona	G	Maryland	W	Pennsylvania	G
Arkansas	G	Massachusetts	W	Puerto Rico	*
California	G	Michigan	W	Rhode Island	W
Colorado	W	Minnesota	W	South Carolina	G & W
Connecticut	W	Mississippi	W	South Dakota	W
Delaware	G	Missouri	W	Tennessee	W
Washington, DC	G	Montana	G	Texas	G
Florida	W	Nebraska	W	Utah	W
Georgia	W	Nevada	G	Vermont	W
Hawaii	W	New Hampshire	W	Virginia	G
Idaho	W	New Jersey	G & W	Washington	W
Illinois	G & W	New Mexico	W	West Virginia	G
Indiana	W	New York	G	Wisconsin	W
Iowa	W	North Carolina	W	Wyoming	W
Kansas	W	North Dakota	G & W		
Kentucky	W	Ohio	W		

Loans Chart

M = Mortgage, a contract by which you promise your property without giving up possession of the property in order to secure a loan. You also retain title to the property.

TD = Trust deed, a contract used as a security device for a loan on your property, by which you transfer bare (naked) legal title with the power of sale to a trustee. This transfer is in effect until you have totally paid off the loan. In the meantime you have possession of the property.

*Mortgage preferred; trust deed also valid.

**Trust deed preferred; mortgage also valid.

***Use note to secure debt.

	LOANS		LOANS		LOANS
Alabama	*M & TD*	Louisiana	*M*	Oklahoma	*M & TD*
Alaska	*M & TD*	Maine	*M*	Oregon	*M & TD*
Arizona	*M & TD*	Maryland	*M & TD*	Pennsylvania	*M*
Arkansas	*M*	Massachusetts	*M*	Puerto Rico	*M*
California	*TD*	Michigan	*M*	Rhode Island	*M*
Colorado	*TD*	Minnesota	*M*	South Carolina	*M & TD*
Connecticut	*M*	Mississippi	*M & TD***	South Dakota	*M*
Delaware	*M*	Missouri	*TD*	Tennessee	*TD*
Washington, DC	*TD*	Montana	*M & TD**	Texas	*TD*
Florida	*M & TD*	Nebraska	*M & TD*	Utah	*M & TD*
Georgia	***	Nevada	*M & TD*	Vermont	*M*
Hawaii	*M*	New Hampshire	*M*	Virginia	*M & TD**
Idaho	*M & TD*	New Jersey	*M*	Washington	*M & TD*
Illinois	*M & TD*	New Mexico	*M & TD*	West Virginia	*TD*
Indiana	*M & TD*	New York	*M*	Wisconsin	*M*
Iowa	*M & TD*	North Carolina	*M & TD*	Wyoming	*M & TD*
Kansas	*M*	North Dakota	*M & TD*		
Kentucky	*M & TD**	Ohio	*M*		

Glossary

Abatement notice A notice to decrease or cease an illegal or unreasonable irritant that hurts, hinders, or damages others or creates a repeated or persisting interference with another's right.

Abstract of title A summary of the history of ownership of a property from public records. This history includes all changes of ownership and claims against the property.

Acceleration clause A provision in a loan document that makes the balance owed on a loan due and payable immediately after a specified event occurs. The event may be missing a payment or violating another provision of the loan.

Acknowledgment A formal declaration before a public official that one has signed a specific document.

Adjustable rate loan Adjustable rate mortgage, ARM; a loan that allows adjustments in the interest rate at specified times based on a named index.

Adjustable rate mortgage *See* Adjustable rate loan.

Adjusted basis The original cost plus capital improvements minus depreciation. Use adjusted basis to compute taxable gain or loss on the sale of a home.

Adjusted sales price As a seller, the price for which you sell your home minus closing costs and commission, if applicable.

Agent A person authorized by another, the principal, to act for him or her in dealing with third parties.

AITD *See* All inclusive trust deed.

Alienation clause *See* Due-on-sale clause.

All inclusive trust deed Wraparound mortgage, AITD; a junior (second, third, and so forth) loan (mortgage or trust deed) at one overall interest rate used to wrap the existing loans into a package. The amount is sufficient to cover the existing loans and provide additional funds for the sellers. Sellers pay on existing loans from buyers' payments. Sellers remain primarily responsible for the original loans.

Amortization Gradual paying off of the principal on a loan by payment of regular installments of principal and interest.

Annual percentage rate APR; an interest rate that includes interest, discount points, origination fees, and loan broker's commission.

Appraisal An examination of a property by a qualified professional to estimate the property's market value as of a specific date.

APR *See* Annual Percentage Rate.

Arbitration Taking of a controversy to an unbiased third person. This person holds a hearing at which both parties may speak and then issues an opinion.

ARM *See* Adjustable rate loan.

Assessment Tax or charge by a governmental body for a specific public improvement covering the property owner's portion of costs. Assessments are in addition to normal property taxes.

Assign Transfer.

Assignee   The person to whom interest is transferred.

Assignment   Transfer of any property to another. Delegation of duties and rights to another.

Assignor   The person from whom interest is transferred.

Assume   Buyers taking over primary responsibility for payment of existing loan. Sellers then become secondarily liable for the loan and for any deficiency judgment.

Assumption fee   The fee a lender may charge for work involved in allowing buyers to assume primary liability for payment on an existing loan.

Attorney   A person licensed to practice law by giving legal advice or assistance, as well as prosecuting and defending cases in courts.

Authorization to sell   A listing contract allowing a real estate professional to act as an agent in the sale of property.

Bankruptcy   Relief by a court of an obligation to pay money owed after turning over all property to a court-appointed trustee.

Basis   The cost of a home when purchased, including down payment, loans, and closing costs.

Beneficiary   The lender of money on a property used in a trust deed type of loan.

Beneficiary statement   A statement provided by a lender using a trust deed type of loan that usually lists claims that do not appear on loan documents.

Bill of lading   A contract for the transportation of your goods with a commercial moving company.

Binder   An informal contract listing an agreement's main points, later replaced by a formal, detailed written contract.

Breach of contract   Failure to perform as promised without a legal excuse (a good reason).

Bridge loan   A short-term loan to buyers who are simultaneously selling one house and trying to buy another.

Broker   *See* Real estate broker.

Building codes   Regulations by governments giving requirements and standards for structures built in their jurisdictions.

Building permits   County-issued documents that permit you to build after your plans have been approved by the necessary city and county agencies.

Buyer's agent   Selling agent; a real estate broker or sales associate who represents the buyer in a transaction.

Buyer's broker   A real estate broker who represents the buyer.

Buyer's fees   Charges that are paid for by the buyers.

Buyer's market   A condition in which there are more sellers than buyers; prices generally decrease.

Call   Demand payment of a debt.

Capital asset   Property, both real and personal, held by a taxpayer and not excluded by tax laws.

Capital gain   Profit from selling or exchanging a capital asset in excess of the cost.

Capital improvements   Additions to property that are permanent, increase property value, and have a useful life of more than one year.

Capital loss   Loss from selling or exchanging property other than a personal residence at less than its cost.

Cashier's check   A bank's own check guaranteed to be good by the bank at which it is drawn.

Casualty   Loss of or damage to structures or personal property.

Casualty insurance   *See* Hazard insurance.

Certificate of title   A report, produced by a party providing abstracts of titles, stating that based on an examination of public records, the title is properly vested in the present owner.

CC&Rs   Covenants, conditions, and restrictions; a document listing private restrictions on property. Often used when buyers have an interest in common areas.

Classified advertisements   Advertisements that are separated by type and listed accordingly.

Closing   Closing escrow, settlement; the final phase of a real estate transaction that involves signing loan documents, paying closing costs, and delivering the deed.

Closing costs   Costs of sale; the additional expenses over and above the purchase price of buying and selling real estate.

Closing escrow   *See* Closing.

Closing fee   *See* Closing.

Closing statement   A written, itemized account given to both seller and buyers at closing by the escrow holder and detailing receipts, disbursements, charges, credits, and prorations.

Commitment   An oral or written agreement to make a loan made by a lender to a potential buyer.

Competent person   A person who meets certain criteria set by a state for competency. These laws often include being a natural person who is an adult or an emancipated minor, mentally competent, and not a felon deprived of civil rights; an artificial person may also meet the requirements.

Commission   Payments to an agent, such as a real estate broker, for services in the selling or buying of a home.

Completion bond   A bond ensuring that if a contractor does not complete a project, an insurance company will pay for the remaining work to be done.

Completion notice   Copy of the document you file and record with your county when work on your home is complete; it places time limits for mechanic's liens.

Condemnation   The act of taking private property for public use after payment of a fair price (compensation).

Conditions   Requirements that must precede the performance or effectiveness of something else. Provisions or qualifications in a deed that if violated or not performed nullify the deed.

Condominium   An undivided ownership in common in a portion of a piece of real property plus a separate interest in space in a building.

Consideration   Anything of value that influences a person to enter into a contract including money, a deed, an item of personal property, an act (including the payment of money), a service, or a promise (such as to pay on a loan). Acts or services must be performed *after* you and the buyers enter into the contract.

Contingency   A condition on which a valid contract depends.

Contingency release   Wipe-out clause, kick-out provision; provisions providing that you will continue to market your home *until* you receive another offer to purchase your home that does *not* contain the contingencies you indicated *or* buyers remove those contingencies you specified. After you receive a contract without the detailed contingencies, the original buyers have the specified time you agreed on to remove the contingencies *or* you may sell your home to the buyers who offered you a contract without the contingencies.

Contract for deed   *See* Land sales contract.

Controller's deed   *See* Tax deed.

Conventional loan   A loan that is not guaranteed or insured by a government agency.

Convey   Transfer.

Costs of sale   *See* Closing costs.

Counteroffer   A statement by a person to whom an offer is made proposing a new offer to the original offeror.

Counterparts   Two documents considered as one.

Covenants   Agreements or promises contained in and conveyed by a deed that are inseparable from the property. Pledges for the performance or nonperformance of certain acts or the use or nonuse of property.

Credit report   A detailed report of a person's credit history and rating.

Dedication   A giving of land by a property owner to the public for public use.

Deed   A document containing a detailed written description of the property that transfers property ownership.

Deed of trust   *See* Trust deed.

Default   Failure of a person to fulfill an obligation or perform a duty; failure to make a loan payment when it is due.

Deficiency judgment   A court decision making an individual personally liable for payoff of a remaining amount due because the full amount was not obtained by foreclosure.

Delinquent payment   A payment that was not paid when it was due.

Demand fee   Demand for payoff charge; a fee for a written request to a lender for lender's demand for payment of the loan in full and the supporting documents necessary for release of the lien against the property.

Demand for payoff charge   *See* Demand fee.

Deposit   Money that buyers submit with a purchase offer as evidence of their intention and ability to buy.

Depreciation   Loss in value from any cause.

Disclosure   Making known things that were previously unknown.

Discount points   *See* Points.

Discovery   Disclosure of things previously unknown.

Discrimination   Giving or withholding particular advantages to or from certain types of persons arbitrarily selected from a larger group. Treating other persons unfairly or denying them normal privileges.

Display advertisements   Large advertisements that often contain illustrations.

Divided agency   Agent's action in representing both parties in a transaction without the knowledge and consent of both.

Documentary transfer tax   *See* Transfer tax.

Down payment   Money that you and buyers agree on, or that a lender requires, that buyers pay toward the purchase price before escrow can close.

Drawing deed fee   A fee for the preparation of a deed.

Dual agent   A broker acting either directly, or through an associate licensee, as agent for both seller and buyer.

Due-on-sale clause   Alienation clause; an acceleration clause in a loan giving the lender the right to demand all sums owed due at once and payable if the property owner transfers title.

Earnest money   *See* Deposit.

Easement   The right a property owner has to use the land of another for a special purpose. It may be valid even if unidentified, unlocated, unmentioned, and unrecorded.

Emancipated minor   A person who is under the age to legally be an adult in the state in which they live but who has some other criteria that allow them to function as adults. The criteria may include being lawfully married or divorced, on duty in the armed forces, or emancipated by court order.

Eminent domain   Governments' power that allows them to take private property for public use after paying what they feel to be a fair price.

Encumbrance   A charge, claim, or lien against a property or personal right or interest in a property that affects or limits the title but does not prevent transfer.

Equity   The part of a property's current value that is owned and on which no money is owed; the property's value minus the liens owed against the property.

Escrow   A process in the transfer of real property in which buyers and sellers deposit documents or money with a neutral third party (the escrow holder). Buyers and sellers give instructions to the escrow holder to hold and deliver documents and money if certain conditions are met.

Escrow instructions   A written agreement between seller and buyers that extrapolates the purchase contract into a form used as directions on how to conduct and close the escrow.

Exclusive agency listing   A listing with only one agency that provides that if the real estate professional obtains the buyer, you must pay the broker the commission. If you sell your home yourself, you are not liable for the commission.

Exclusive right to sell listing   A listing providing that, during the time listed, only that broker has the right to sell your home and earn the commission no matter who makes the sale.

Extended coverage title insurance   This coverage protects against numerous risks that are not a matter of record.

FHA   Federal Housing Administration; a federal governmental agency that manages FHA-insured loans to protect lenders in case of default by buyers.

FHA loan   Financing by having a conventional loan made by a lender and insured by the Federal Housing Administration.

Fiduciary   A person who is in a position of trust who must act in the best interest of clients.

Fire insurance   *See* Hazard insurance.

Flood Hazard Area Disclosure   A federally required disclosure to inform buyers that the property is located in a region designated as a special flood hazard area.

Fixed rate loan   A loan on which the percentage of interest remains at the same rate over the life of the loan. The payments of principal remain equal during the entire period.

Fixture   Items permanently attached to or for which special openings were made in a home and its associated structures.

Fix-up costs   The expenses of improvements, repairs, and attractiveness items.

Flyers   Leaflets for mass distribution.

Foreclosure   The process by which a property on which a borrower has not paid is sold to satisfy a loan against the property.

Fraud   Willfully concealing or misrepresenting a material fact in order to influence another person to take action. The action results in the person's loss of property or legal rights.

FSBO   For sale by owner; a phrase describing a home owner selling property without using a real estate broker.

Geological inspection   Inspection for potential or actual geological problems, as well as examination of records to determine whether property falls within any special zones.

Gift deed   A deed given for love and affection.

GI loan   *See* VA loan.

Grant deed   A deed using the word *grant* in the clause that transfers ownership.

Grantee   Buyer; receiver of a title to a property.

Grantor   Seller; holder of a title to a property.

Guarantee of title   A warranty that title is vested in the party shown on the deed.

Hazard insurance   Casualty insurance, fire insurance; insurance protection against stated specific hazards such as fire, hail, windstorms, earthquakes, floods, civil disturbances, explosions, riots, theft, and vandalism.

Home equity line of credit   Credit given by a lender based on the amount of one's equity in a property. The line of credit becomes a loan secured by a mortgage or trust deed when the borrower uses some or all of the credit.

Home inspection   *See* Physical inspection.

Home inspector   A qualified person who examines and reports on the general condition of a home's site and structures.

Homeowner's association dues   Monthly fees owners of homes pay to their home owner's association for the items it provides.

Homeowner's insurance   A policy protecting a homeowner from liability and casualty hazards listed in the policy.

Home protection plan   *See* Home warranty.

Home warranty   Home protection plan; insurance that items listed are in working order for the specified length of time.

Impounds   Reserve fund; funds held by the lender to assure payment in the future of recurring expenses. These expenses can include insurance premiums and taxes.

Improper delivery Delivery of a deed that has not passed out of seller's control and/or was not delivered to buyers during the seller's lifetime.

Improvement costs Expenses for permanent additions.

Improvement notices Documents sent by governments giving notice of one-time charges for planned improvements (e.g., sidewalks).

Imputed interest rate The minimum rate the IRS requires for a seller-financed loan. If you charge less than the minimum rate the IRS taxes you on the minimum.

Index A measurement of interest rates on which changes in interest charges on adjustable rate loans are based.

Inspection records Notices indicating that inspections have been conducted by the proper local authorities at certain specified points in the building process.

Inspection reports Reports by inspectors about the condition of various aspects of your property, including defects and repairs considered necessary.

Installment note A loan paid back in at least two payments of principal on different dates.

Installment sale A sale that allows the seller to receive payments in more than one tax year.

Interest A charge or rate paid in arrears (after incurred) to a lender for borrowing money.

Interest-only loan A loan for which only the interest is paid and no principal is repaid until the final installment.

Interpleader action Request by a closing agent or escrow holder that a court take custody of the deposited funds and make a judgment as to their distribution.

Jointly and severally liable Liable along with other parties and personally liable.

Joint tenancy Vesting wherein two or more parties acquire title at the same time. Each party has an equal, undivided interest and equal right to possess the property, including automatic right of survivorship.

Judgment Final determination by a court of a matter presented to it. A general monetary obligation on all property of the person who owes the money. This obligation applies in each county where an abstract of the court judgment was recorded.

Kick-out provision *See* Contingency release.

Lack of capacity Inability to enter into a contract because one is not a competent person by his or her state's criteria.

Landfill Soil moved onto the site from another location.

Landlord The owner or lessor of real property.

Land sales contract Contract for deed, real property sales contract; an agreement in which the seller retains title to property until the buyer performs all contract conditions.

Lease A contract that transfers possession and use of designated property for a limited, stated time under specified conditions.

Lease option A contract that stipulates that potential buyers are leasing a property for an agreed-upon rental payment. These buyers have the right to purchase the property before the specified future date for the amount listed in the contract. Part of the lease payment is considered option money toward the purchase price.

Lease purchase A contract that states that buyers are leasing the property for the agreed-upon amount and conditions. The buyers agree to purchase the property at the agreed-upon time for the agreed-upon amount.

Legal description A formal description giving a property's location, size, and boundaries in written and/or map form.

Lessee The tenant or person who leases property from the landlord in order to use it.

Lessor The landlord or owner of property who leases the property to the tenant for the tenant's use.

Liability Responsibility for damages to other people or property; what you owe against an asset.

Lien A claim against a property making the property security for debts such as loans, mechanic's liens, and taxes.

Lien releases Documents releasing one from monetary liability to the party listed after fully paying that party.

Liquidated damages The amount of money you may keep if the buyers default or breach the contact.

Lis pendens An official recorded notice that legal action is pending against the title to the property.

Listing Authorization to sell; a contract allowing a real estate broker to act as an agent to buy, lease, or sell property for another.

Litigation Lawsuits.

Loan disclosure statement A lender's account summary required by the Federal Truth in Lending Act.

Loan discount fee *See* Points.

Loan fees One-time charges by the lender for initiating a loan, including points, appraisal, and credit report on buyers.

Loan origination fee Lender's charge for arranging and processing a loan, usually based on a percentage of the loan.

Loan tie-in fee A fee charged by whoever handles closing for their work and liability in conforming to the lender's criteria for the buyers' new loan.

Market value The amount buyers are willing to pay and sellers are willing to accept within a reasonable time.

Marshal's deed *See* Sheriff's deed.

Material facts Any facts that if known would influence a person's decision.

Mechanic's lien A claim filed against property by a contractor, service provider, or supplier for work done or materials provided for which full payment has not been received.

MLS *See* Multiple Listing Service.

Mortgage A contract to secure a loan by which you promise your property without giving up possession or title.

Mortgage default insurance Default insurance; insurance coverage enabling the lender to receive a part of the outstanding balance in the event you default.

Mortgage disability insurance Insurance coverage enabling you to pay monthly mortgage charges in the event you are totally and permanently disabled.

Mortgagee Lender of money on property using a mortgage.

Mortgage life insurance Insurance coverage enabling whomever you designate to pay the loan balance if you die.

Mortgagor Property owner who borrows money using a mortgage.

Multiple Listing Service MLS; an agency to which real estate brokers belong in order to pool their listings with other real estate brokers. If a sale is made, the listing and selling brokers share the commission.

Negative amortization Process in which payments on a loan do not cover interest payments and the difference between the payment and interest due are added to the loan balance.

Net listing A listing providing that the broker retain all money received in excess of the price set by the seller.

Nominal interest rate Interest rate stated in a promissory note.

Nonconforming uses Preexisting uses of land allowed to continue even though a current ordinance excluding that use has been enacted for that area.

Notary fee A charge paid to a notary public to witness signatures on some of the legal documents in a transaction.

Notice of default Warning sent to a borrower on a loan cautioning the borrower that the payment is delinquent.

Offset statement A statement regarding a loan provided by the seller when a beneficiary statement is not available.

Open listing   A nonexclusive right-to-sell agreement one can make with one or more real estate professionals. It provides that if you sell your home yourself, you are not liable to the broker for a commission. If, however, a real estate professional obtains the buyers for the property, you must pay the broker the commission you have negotiated.

Option   A contract to keep an offer to buy, sell, or lease property open for a period and under the terms agreed upon.

Optionee   The person who gets the option on a property.

Optionor   The owner of a title who gives an option.

Option to buy   *See* Purchase option.

Payment records   Checks, receipts, and written ledgers.

Payment statements   Monthly stubs showing your payment date, amounts applied to principal and interest, and remaining balance due, as well as annual summary statements.

Permission-to-show listing   A listing contract that allows a real estate professional to show your property only to the person or persons named in that contract. You pay the commission only if someone on the list purchases your home.

Personal property   Items that are not permanently attached to your home or other structures on your property.

Pest control inspection   Structural pest control inspection, termite inspection; inspection for infestation or infection by wood-destroying pests or organisms.

Physical inspection   Home inspection; examination of the general physical condition of a property's site and structures.

Planned unit development   PUD; a subdivision in which the lots are separately owned but other areas are owned in common.

Points   Discount points, loan discount fee; a one-time charge by the lender to adjust the yield on the loan to current market conditions or to adjust the rate on the loan to market rate. Each point is equal to 1 percent of the loan balance.

Power of attorney   A document that gives one person the power to sign documents for another person.

Power of sale clause   A provision in a loan allowing the lender to foreclose and sell borrower's property publicly without a court procedure.

Preliminary title report   Report summarizing the title search performed by a title company or lawyer for a property.

Prepayment penalty   A fine imposed on a borrower by a lender for the early payoff of a loan or any substantial part of a loan.

Principal   One of the parties in a real estate transaction, either you or the buyers.

Principal residence   An IRS term denoting the residence wherein you spend the most time during the tax year.

Probate court   A court that handles wills and the administration of estates of people who have died.

Promissory note   The written contract you sign promising to pay a definite amount of money by a definite future date.

Property taxes   Taxes; taxes assessed on property at a uniform rate so that the amount of the tax depends on the value.

Property tax statements   Documents that the county assessor's office mails to home owners itemizing the semiannual or annual tax bill on a home and indicating the payment due dates.

Prorations   Proportional distributions of responsibility for the payment of the expenses of home ownership. This distribution is based on the percentage of an assessment or billing period during which the seller and buyers own the property.

PUD   *See* Planned unit development.

Purchase contract   The contract containing terms and conditions to which you and the buyers agree when you accept the buyers' offer to purchase your home.

Purchase option   Option to buy; the type of contract in which buyers agree to purchase the property for the amount listed in the contract, *if* they decide to buy your home and make the purchase within the listed period of time, and agree that you keep the option fee *if* they do not buy the property.

Quitclaim deed   A deed using the word *quitclaim* in the clause granting ownership and thus releasing the grantor from any claim to that property. A quitclaim deed has no warranties.

Real estate   *See* Real property.

Real estate broker   A real estate agent who represents another person in dealing with third parties. This person must take required courses, pass a broker's exam, and be state licensed. A broker may employ other qualified individuals and is responsible for their actions.

Real estate professional   A real estate broker or sales associate.

Real estate sales agent   A person who is licensed by a state and who represents a real estate broker in transactions.

Real Estate Settlement Procedures Act   *See* RESPA.

Real property   Real estate; land and whatever is built on, growing on, or attached to the land.

Real property sales contract   *See* Land sales contract.

Reconveyance deed   A deed that records full satisfaction of a trust deed secured debt on your property and transfers bare legal title from the trustee to you.

Recording   Official entry of liens, reconveyances, and transactions into the permanent records of a county.

Release of contract   An agreement that all responsibilities and rights occurring as a result of a contract are invalid.

Repair costs   Expenses for work maintaining a home's condition, including replacement and restoration.

Request for notice of default   A recorded notice allowing a county recorder to notify lenders of foreclosure on a property in which the lender has an interest.

Rescind   To cancel a contract and restore the parties to the state they would have been in had the contract never been made.

Reserve fund   *See* Impounds.

RESPA   Real Estate Settlement Procedures Act; a federal law that requires that buyers be given, in advance of closing, information regarding their loan.

Restrictions   Encumbrances that limit the use of real estate by specifying actions the owner must take or cannot take on or with his or her property.

Revocation   Involuntary cancellation that occurs when the time limit has expired *and* one or both parties do not perform in accordance with the terms of the contract.

Sales associate   A real estate professional with either a broker's or sales license who acts as an agent for a broker.

Satisfaction of mortgage   A document indicating that you have paid your mortgage off in full.

Sale leaseback   An agreement in which the seller sells the property to buyers who agree to lease the property back to the seller.

Seller buy-down loan   A loan in which the effective interest rate is bought down (reduced) during the beginning years of the loan by contributions a seller makes.

Seller carry-back loan   A loan for which the seller acts as a lender to carry back or hold mortgage notes from buyers. These notes may be first, second, or even third loans.

Seller's agent   *See* Listing.

Selling agent   *See* Buyer's agent.

Seller's market   A condition in which there are more buyers than sellers; prices generally increase.

Setback   Laws prohibiting the erection of a building within a certain distance of the curb.

Settlement   *See* Closing.

Settling   Sinking and then coming to rest in one place.

Severalty   Vesting of title in which you hold title by yourself.

Sheriff's deed   Marshal's deed; a deed used by courts in foreclosure or in carrying out a judgment. This deed transfers a debtor's title to a buyer.

Single agent   An agent representing only one party in a real estate transaction.

Sliding   The large downward movement of a soil mass out of its previous position.

Slippage   The small downward movement of a soil mass out of its previous position.

Special endorsements   Specific endorsements that modify, expand, or delete the coverage of any insurance policy.

Special Studies Zone Disclosure   A form used to inform buyers that a property is in an area specified as a Special Studies Zone by California law. These zones primarily affect areas where there was or may be serious earthquake destruction.

Specific performance   Law that allows one party to sue another to perform as specified under the terms of their contract.

Standard coverage title insurance   The regular investigation for this insurance generally reveals only matters of record and location of the improvements with respect to the lot line.

Straight note   A promise to pay a loan in which the principal is paid as one lump sum, although the interest may be paid in one lump sum or in installments.

Subescrow fee   A fee charged by some escrow holders for their costs when they handle money.

Subject-to loan   An existing loan for which buyers take over responsibility for the payments, and seller remains primarily liable in the event of a deficiency judgment.

Survey fee   A fee charged for a survey showing the exact location and boundaries of a property.

Take sheet   A form used to collect information necessary to prepare the escrow instructions.

Tax deed   Controller's deed; a deed used by a state to transfer title to the buyers.

Taxes   *See* Property taxes.

Tax preparers   Persons who prepare tax returns.

Tax stamps   A method of denoting that a transfer tax has been paid in which stamps are affixed to a deed before the deed may be recorded.

Telephone register   A listing of information regarding telephone calls you receive.

Termination of agency   Ending of an agency agreement.

Time is of the essence   A statement that one party in a contract must perform certain acts within the stated period before the other party can perform.

Title   Evidence of one's right to a property and the extent of that right.

Title insurance   The policy issued to you by the title company on completion of the final title search protecting against claims in the future based on circumstances in the past.

Title insurance companies   Companies issuing title insurance policies.

Title search   An examination of information recorded on your property at the county recorder's office. This examination verifies that the property has no outstanding claims or liens against it to adversely affect the buyer or lender and that you can transfer clear legal title to the property.

Transfer fee   *See* Assumption fee.

Transfer tax   Documentary transfer tax; a tax that some states allow individual counties or cities to place on the transferring of real property.

Trust deed   A document, used as a security device for the loan on your property, by which you transfer bare (naked) legal title with the power of sale to a trustee. This transfer is in effect until you have totally paid off the loan.

Trustee   A person who holds bare legal title to a property without being the actual owner of the property. The trustee has the power of sale for the lender's benefit.

Trustee's deed A deed used by a trustee in a foreclosure handled outside of court to transfer the debtor's title to buyers.

Trust funds Funds held by a closing agent or escrow holder for the benefit of the buyers or seller.

Truth in lending A federal law that requires disclosure of loan terms to a borrower who is using his or her principal residence as security for a loan.

Unconditional lien release Waiver of liens; a release, usually signed by a contractor, after a job is complete and you made the final payments waiving and releasing all rights and claims against your home.

Unenforceable Not able to be enforced; void.

Unlawful detainer The unjustifiable keeping of possession of real property by someone who originally had the right to possession but no longer has that right.

Unmarketability of title Inability to sell property because of unacceptable encumbrances and liens on the title.

Usury Interest charged in excess of what state law permits.

VA Veterans Administration; the federal government agency that manages VA loans.

VA loan GI loan; financing made by having a conventional loan made by a lender guaranteed by the Veterans Administration.

Variance An approved release from current zoning regulations regarding the use or alteration of property.

Vendee Purchaser or buyer.

Vendor Owner or seller.

Vesting Interest that cannot be revoked.

Veterans Administration *See* VA.

Void To have no effect; unenforceable at law.

Voidable Able to be set aside.

Waive Unilateral voluntary relinquishment of a right of which one is aware.

Waiver of liens *See* Unconditional lien release.

Walk-through inspection Buyers' physical examination of a property within a few days before closing verifying that systems, appliances, and the house itself are in the agreed-upon condition.

Warranties Printed or written documents guaranteeing the condition of property or its components.

Warranty deed A deed in which the grantor explicitly guarantees the title to be as indicated in the deed. The grantor agrees to protect buyers against all claimants to the property.

Waiver of liens *See* Unconditional lien release.

Wipe-out clause *See* Contingency release.

Work stoppage clause A clause in a contract giving a contractor the right to stop work if you do not make the required payments.

Wraparound mortgage *See* All inclusive trust deed.

Zoning Governmental laws establishing building codes and governing the specific uses of land and buildings.

Index